University of Michigan Business School Management Series

INNOVATIVE SOLUTIONS TO THE PRESSING PROBLEMS OF BUSINESS

The mission of the University of Michigan Business School Management Series is to provide accessible, practical, and cutting-edge solutions to the most critical challenges facing businesspeople today. The UMBS Management Series provides concepts and tools for people who seek to make a significant difference in their organizations. Drawing on the research and experience of faculty at the University of Michigan Business School, the books are written to stretch thinking while providing practical, focused, and innovative solutions to the pressing problems of business.

Executive Summary

Creating value is the raison d'être for both organizations and individuals. Organizations that create more value than their peers deliver superior bottom-line financial results and win the competitive game of dominance in the marketplace. Individuals who create more value than their peers earn the trust and respect of their organizations and increase their own value in the employment marketplace. In short, bottom-line business success for both organizations and individuals can be defined as sustained value creation.

Unfortunately, while most people want to create value for themselves and their organizations, many well-intentioned efforts to manage individual and functional-area responsibilities actually destroy value for the organization as a whole. This book analyzes the forces that lead to value destruction and shows how to combat them at both the organizational and individual levels.

Sustained value creation depends on a mastery of the five secrets of great value creators introduced in Chapter One: (1) understanding the meaning of value, both to individuals and to the organization; (2) developing a deep understanding of the multiple and sometimes conflicting perspectives on value creation that exist in any organization; (3) understanding the organization's strategy for success and developing a personal success strategy that supports it; (4) developing the appropriate measures of success; and (5) mastering speed.

Chapters Two and Three develop these secrets of sustained value creation in depth. The remaining chapters demonstrate how to operationalize the basic principles of value creation in the various functional areas in a typical organization: Procurement and Manufacturing (Chapter Four); Marketing, Sales and Distribution, and New Product Development (Chapter Five); Human Resources (Chapter Six); and Finance (Chapter Seven). Individuals will come away from these chapters with a better understanding of the perspectives of those in other functional areas as well as specific strategies and tools for helping to sustain and enhance value creation both for themselves and for the organization as a whole.

Becoming a
Better Value
Creator

How to Improve the
Company's Bottom Line—
and Your Own

Anjan V. Thakor

JOSSEY-BASS
A Wiley Company
San Francisco

Manufactured in the United States of America on Lyons Falls Turin Book. This paper is acid-free and 100 percent totally chlorine-free.

Library of Congress Cataloging-in-Publication Data

Thakor, Anjan V.
   Becoming a better value creator: how to improve the company's bottom line—and your own / Anjan V. Thakor.—1st ed.
      p. cm.—(The University of Michigan Business School management series)
   Includes index.
   ISBN 0-7879-5308-3 (acid-free paper)
   1. Industrial management. 2. Value analysis (Cost control) I. Title. II. Series.
   HD31 .T483 2000
   658.15—dc21   00-009555

FIRST EDITION

HB Printing   10 9 8 7 6 5 4 3 2 1

Contents

I'd like to dedicate this book to my family,
Serry, Richard, and Cullen, and my dear friend and
mentor, Stuart Greenbaum, who has been a constant
source of sage advice and inspiration.

Foreword

Welcome to the University of Michigan Business School Management Series. The books in this series address the most urgent problems facing business today. The series is part of a larger initiative at the University of Michigan Business School (UMBS) that ties together a range of efforts to create and share knowledge through conferences, survey research, interactive and distance training, print publications, and new media.

It is just this type of broad-based initiative that sparked my love affair with UMBS in 1984. From the day I arrived I was en- amored with the quality of the research, the quality of the MBA program, and the quality of the Executive Education Center. Here was a business school committed to new lines of research, new ways of teaching, and the practical application of ideas. It was a place where innovative thinking could result in tangible outcomes.

The UMBS Management Series is one very important outcome, and it has an interesting history. It turns out that every year five thousand participants in our executive program fill out a marketing survey in which they write statements indicating the most important problems they face. One day Lucy Chin, one of our administrators, handed me a document containing all these statements. A content analysis of the data resulted in a list of forty-five pressing problems. The topics ranged from growing a company to managing personal stress. The list covered a wide territory, and I started to see its potential. People in organizations tend to be driven by a very traditional set of problems, but the solutions evolve. I went to my friends at Jossey-Bass to discuss a publishing project. The discussion eventually grew into the University of Michigan Business School Management Series— Innovative Solutions to the Pressing Problems of Business.

The books are independent of each other, but collectively they create a comprehensive set of management tools that cut across all the functional areas of business—from strategy to human resources to finance, accounting, and operations. They draw on the interdisciplinary research of the Michigan faculty. Yet each book is written so a serious manager can read it quickly and act immediately. I think you will find that they are books that will make a significant difference to you and your organization.

Robert E. Quinn, Consulting Editor
M.E. Tracy Distinguished Professor
University of Michigan Business School

Preface

Much of my recent work has focused on helping organizations improve their financial performance—or, in the terms used in this book, showing them how they can maximize sustained value creation. So I was delighted but not surprised when my friend and colleague Bob Quinn asked me if I would consider writing a book on how corporations can "improve their bottom line" as part of the University of Michigan Business School Management Series.

My research, teaching, and consulting are in the areas of corporate finance, banking, and strategy—and I must admit that when I first agreed to this project, my intention was to focus on the financial strategies that firms could employ to boost performance. However, as I began to systematically sort through my own research data as well as the work of others, the way I visualized the book changed dramatically. I became convinced that real value creation in organizations is related as much to the way each individual in the organization behaves as it is to financial strategies. In every organization, there are forces that work to destroy value despite everyone's best intentions about improving the bottom line. But overcoming these forces and sustaining real value creation depends on the way each employee translates corporate strategy into a personal plan for constructive change, the way each employee takes owner-ship of the organizational assets he or she manages.

With this shift in focus, the main question I wanted to pursue was obvious: What makes organizations and individuals effective value creators? That is the question this book attempts to answer.

I believe that understanding the secrets of value creation is not only more important today than it was in the past, but will become increasingly important in the future. Why? There are two reasons.

First, during the Industrial Age, the focus on creating value was on improving organizational processes. Mass-manufacturing economies of scale, efficiencies garnered through hyperefficient distribution systems, Six-Sigma quality control programs, and so on all contributed to enormous value creation in organizations. We will continue to see organizations get progressively better at designing and managing processes to improve efficiency. But such initiatives no longer have breakthrough value-creation potential. We are already witnessing diminishing marginal returns when it comes to the incremental value creation possible through improving efficiency. Meanwhile, in the Information Age, we are beginning to see the enormous power of the individual in driving value creation. The reason is that the competitive dynamics in most industries are evolving in a highly nonlinear way, with frequent breaks or discontinuities from the past, and adapting effectively to such chaos requires individual creativity rather than just the linear discipline of an efficient organizational process. Those organizations with the best value creators rather than the best *managers* (those most skilled in managing well-defined organizational processes) are the best positioned to thrive in the future. So if you want to ensure the success of your organization in this new environment, you'd be well advised to seek out the value creators and to understand the organizational dynamics that either enhance or diminish value creation. Second, as the economy expands at a rapid clip, creating new industries and new organizations almost overnight, the demand for individual value creators is growing exponentially. Organizations are prepared to pay such individuals at levels that would have seemed almost astronomical just a short time ago. Smaller Internet start-ups, where the perceived value creation opportunities are the greatest, are able to attract outstanding individuals from Fortune 500 companies. The demand for individual value creators is unprecedented. So if you want to improve your own "bottom line" as an individual, you should learn the secrets of those who have figured out how to be effective value creators.

This book is a pragmatic guide to understanding and mastering the tools of value creation. Although it is based on extensive research into organizational and personal effectiveness, it is not written for academics. Rather, it is designed to aid both individuals and organizations become more effective at creating value. The expositional style of the book, the numerous case studies of actual companies, and the end-of-chapter exercises are all intended to help readers develop useful and practical skills.

Who should read this book? There are many groups that could benefit from the ideas and strategies presented here. Senior executives can use this book as a self-improvement guide. More important, they can encourage those in their organizations to read the book and thereby improve their value contribution. Educating employees in value creation will facilitate a more effective leveraging of the human resources in the organization and elevate its bottom-line potential by combating the value-destroying effects of functional silos, which the book analyzes in depth. CEOs and Boards of Directors can use the book to evaluate the value-creation abilities of those below them. Entrepreneurs can use it to determine the optimal human resource strategies for the organizations they are developing. In short, anybody who is interested in improving their own bottom line as well as that of their organization should expect to find something of value in this book.

As someone who has researched, taught, and consulted on finance and strategy issues for many years, I have come to deeply appreciate the importance of the individual in driving organizational value creation. I have also come to appreciate the enormous dissipation of this value-creation potential that occurs routinely either because employees lack a sense of personal ownership of the assets they manage or because they simply don't know what it takes to be an effective value creator. Such value dissipation is pure waste. It doesn't help the individual feel personally fulfilled. It doesn't help the organization realize its value-creation potential. And it doesn't benefit society. My hope is that the tools developed in this book will guide individuals to become more valuable to their organizations and to achieve a greater sense of personal fulfillment. Here's wishing you the best, value creators!

May 2000   Anjan V. Thakor
Ann Arbor, Michigan

The Five Secrets of
Great Value Creators

D o you ever wonder why some people you know are getting ahead faster than others of seemingly similar abilities? Do you ever wonder why some people are happier
in their jobs than others? Why is it that some people seem to
have so much more energy and enthusiasm for their work than
those around them?

And why is it that some organizations consistently outperform others, often within the same industry? Why is there a single high school in Japan that, over the years, has produced the
most Olympic champions, the largest percentage of students
going to college, and the largest number of leaders of Japanese
industry?

Among the many possible answers to these questions, two stand out. Individuals who get ahead the fastest, have the greatest energy and enthusiasm, and are the happiest typically are those who are the most effective value creators. And the organizations that consistently outperform others are those with the most effective value-creating individuals. Jack Welch, CEO of General Electric, once said, "If you're not thinking all the time about making every person more valuable, you don't have a chance."

In effect, creating value is the reason for being for both individuals and organizations. At a personal level, value creation—having a positive impact on something that matters to us—is one of the most basic human goals. Creating value is how we achieve self-fulfillment and realize our unique potential.

As individuals, we can create value in many dimensions: for our families, for our friends, for the organizations we work for, and for society. Although this book focuses on how to become a better value creator in an organization, the principles it develops can be applied more broadly.

Like every individual, every organization exists to create value, be it a corporation, a church, a school, or a government. What represents value differs, though, from one organization to another. For a publicly traded company like IBM, value is linked to the financial returns the company delivers for its shareholders. For a nonprofit educational institution, value may be linked to some measure of the quality of students' educational experience. As an individual value creator, you need to understand the value-creation context of your organization, and your specific role in it. As a manager or executive who bears responsibility for increasing value in the organization, you need to know the factors that create and destroy value at the organizational level.

■ The Meaning of Value Creation

What do I mean by value creation, and why is it so central? Let me begin with you as an individual. There is only one reason why you are employed by the organization you work for: the value of the benefits you produce for the organization exceeds the cost to the organization of having you produce those benefits. The cost to the organization includes your wages and other compensation as well as what it costs to provide you with the resources you need to do your job. Thus, for any given period,

Value created by you = Value of the organizational
benefits you produce
– Direct (tangible) cost of employing you
(wages, perquisites, and so on)
– Opportunity cost to the organization of the
labor and capital resources you use in your work

Viewed in this perspective, you create value for the organization when the value of what you produce exceeds the value of what you consume. You will thus create more value if you can increase the flow of benefits you are producing for the organization or reduce the organizational resources you consume to produce the same level of benefits. When you do this, you become more valuable to your organization. As a result you may be paid more, gain more respect from colleagues, improve your chances for promotion, or increase your market value and hence your job mobility and satisfaction. If you are a deficit producer, you can expect to be terminated or encouraged to leave voluntarily. Your value to the organization is directly related to the magnitude of the surplus you produce.

Similarly, an organization creates value if the products and services that it produces have a greater value to its customers than the organizational costs of producing these products and services. For a profit-seeking organization, this will translate into something like *Economic Value*, that is, revenues less tangible costs less the opportunity cost of capital resources (property, plant, equipment, working capital, and so on) used to produce revenue.

For a nonprofit community service organization, a similar notion of value would apply, but revenue would need to be replaced by some measure of the value of the community services rendered by the organization. The important point is that even for such an organization, value creation would not be judged in isolation from the resources (human, financial, community infrastructure, and so on) consumed to produce the services.

This book presents innovative approaches to becoming a more effective value creator in your organization, as well as strategies to help your organization consistently maximize its value-creation potential. It offers a simple explanation of why people often fail to create value, even though that is what they mean to do, and it describes the tools for creating value and avoiding inadvertent value destruction.

It turns out that there are five keys to becoming a great value creator. If you master these keys, you will open doors to personal and organizational success that previously seemed shut tight. At the organizational level, maximizing value means achieving the goals expected by shareholders, sponsors, or other stakeholders—in short, fulfilling the organization's mission.

■ Introducing the Five Secrets

To introduce the five secrets of great value creators, let me begin with a story. A few years ago, I was working at another university. We were having considerable difficulty hiring and retaining good secretaries to provide faculty support. The university's pay structure wasn't very good, and as faculty members we had virtually no ability to reward secretaries for exceptional performance. Consequently, the secretaries did what was expected of them and no more. And as long as the faculty were reasonably satisfied, it was a job well done.

We then hired a secretary who changed all that. She was different from the start. First, in addition to learning what her job responsibilities were, she wanted to know all about what I did—in effect, how value was created for the organization. Although I was surprised at first by her questions, I eventually realized what she was doing. As someone who supported me, she wanted to know what she could do to make me more effective, to increase my value creation. Once she understood this, she redefined her job. Rather than taking her job description as a given, she created a new job that was more fun and satisfying for her—one that was a better developmental experience for her and more valuable for me and the organization.

Another remarkable thing about my secretary was that she was always eager to learn new ways to improve the quality of her output. And she was never shy about telling the faculty members she worked for how they could do something better. This again was something I had to get used to, but it wasn't hard because she often made good suggestions.

Finally, there wasn't a deadline she couldn't meet. The faster she worked, the happier she was. The expectations she had of her own performance always seemed to exceed the expectations anyone else had of her.

Illustrated in this simple story are some of the visible outcomes that all value creators seem to produce. As an outstanding value creator:

- You add more value to the organization than is expected.
- You expect more of yourself than anyone else does and help to reinvent your own job into one that is more fulfilling and enjoyable for you, creates greater value for the organization, and changes the organization around you.
- You are more fun for your colleagues to be around.
- You use speed as a key asset.
- You not only become more valuable to your existing organization, you become more marketable and gain greater job mobility.

How do you produce these outcomes? To be a great value creator, you need to know the answers to five groups of questions:

1. What does *value* mean to your organization? To you?
2. What are all the activities your organization is involved in to create value? What activities are you engaged in to create value?
3. What is your organization's strategy? What is your personal strategy in the organization?
4. How do you and your organization measure success? How do you, personally, set your own expectations?
5. How fast are you at creating value? What can you do to improve speed without compromising quality?

Each of these sets of questions correspond to one of the five keys to creating value: the "secrets" of great value creators (Figure 1.1). And each also corresponds to a set of pitfalls and a set of tools for both individuals and organizations.

What Does *Value* Mean to You and Your Organization?

As I noted earlier, the nature of the business an organization is involved in determines what the definition of value for that organization. Before you can become an effective value creator, you must first understand what constitutes value in your organization.

The Importance of Understanding the Meaning of Value
Why is this clear view of the meaning of value so important? Consider a simple example. Suppose you are working as a loan officer in a bank with the goal of maximizing its Economic Value. (For a publicly traded company, *Economic Value* can be thought of as shareholder value.) In this case, all your lending decisions should be based on whether they will increase the bank's Economic Value. You will not always accommodate the

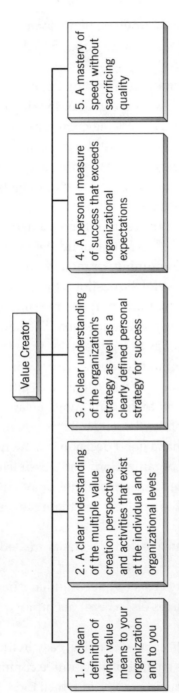

Figure 1.1. The Five Secrets of Value Creators

Value Creator

1. A clean definition of what value means to your organization and to you

2. A clear understanding of the multiple value creation perspectives and activities that exist at the individual and organizational levels

3. A clear understanding of the organization's strategy as well as a clearly defined personal strategy for success

4. A personal measure of success that exceeds organizational expectations

5. A mastery of speed without sacrificing quality

□

credit needs of your borrowers. Some loan requests will be rejected because the loans would not add to the bank's Economic Value.

But now imagine you are doing the same work in a cooperative organization with the goal of making its members collectively better off and enhancing community development. You would now care not just about the bottom line but also about whether you were making a loan applicant and the community better off. So, whereas the profit-maximizing bank might turn down a loan request from a real estate developer who wanted to build low-income houses or refurbish a depressed downtown area, you might well decide to extend the loan as a loan officer at the cooperative community organization.

Note that this is not a question of who is right and who is wrong. Both organizations may be maximizing value, even though they make opposite decisions. The bank may view the loan to the developer as being too risky, given its credit-quality standards. The community cooperative organization, by contrast, has a different definition of value that takes into account the benefit of the development to the community at large, rather than just its risk-adjusted profit to the lender. How you interpret the word *value* determines what a good decision is in a given situation.

The variety of organizations and possible notions of value is very large. Yet the same general notion of value creation that was introduced earlier applies to all these organizations, namely,

Value created = Benefits created
– Direct costs
– Opportunity costs (what could have been earned
by using resources elsewhere) of employing resources

Quantifying benefits created is not as easy in the case of not-for-profit organizations such as a cooperative community bank as it is for a profit-maximizing entity, in which these benefits are typically measured as revenue. But that is a measurement issue rather than a basic problem in defining value creation. The challenge for not-for-profit organizations is to first determine all of the ways in which the organization creates value and then find measures of these different values.

This book will focus primarily on profit-maximizing organizations. For such organizations, value created can be defined more specifically as follows:

Economic Value (also called *Economic Value Added*) = Revenue
  – Direct costs (including taxes)
  – Opportunity cost of using capital = After-tax profit
  – Opportunity cost of using capital

Note that this follows from the earlier notion of Value Created. *Revenue* represents the benefits created; *Direct costs* include a variety of costs such as labor, materials, electricity, marketing, and so on, and *Opportunity cost* of capital is what the providers of capital would have earned had they invested their capital elsewhere.

If the organization is a publicly traded company, another commonly used measure of value creation is *shareholder returns*, that is, the returns received by shareholders in any given period through price appreciation and dividends. A closely related measure is market value added (MVA), which is the difference between the market value of the firm (derived from its per-share stock price) and its book value. It turns out that, over time, average Economic Value is fairly highly correlated with average MVA. Since Economic Value can be used for both publicly traded and privately held firms, it will serve as a value creation measure for this book.

Two Levels of Understanding: Organizational and Personal
There are two levels to the concept of value creation. The first is organizational: what does it mean for your organization to be

successful at creating value? The second is personal: how do *you* create value?

My research shows that a deep understanding of value creation is usually lacking at both levels. At the organizational level, many managers tend to think of value creation in terms of the stock price or earnings per share, without grasping the difference between value creation and *sustained* value creation. The goal of any organization should be sustained value creation. This means making decisions that are in the long-term interests of all the stakeholders—shareholders, employees, and customers—rather than maximizing short-term profits or the stock price.

To contribute to your organization's success, you also need to understand how you yourself create value. This means knowing the answers to three questions:

1. What are the key value drivers you control?
2. How do these value drivers affect some measure of value that is relevant at levels above your own in the organization?
3. What innovations in the management of these drivers can you introduce?

A value driver is simply a decision variable that affects or promotes the creation of value. If you are a plant manager in charge of Manufacturing, for example: your key value drivers might include such things as the quality of the training received by your factory employees, the innate talent of these employees, the complexity of your manufacturing processes, and the design of the factory. In subsequent chapters you will see many examples of value drivers in various functional areas.

Note that value drivers are not outcomes—they are the determinants of outcomes. In the case of the plant manager, the outcomes are things like manufacturing cycle time, product quality as measured by defects, and manufacturing cost per unit. These outcomes are affected by the value drivers the plant manager controls. Rather than focusing on the outcomes, the plant manager needs to focus on the drivers that influence these outcomes.

Answering the three questions about value drivers just listed is difficult for a variety of reasons. For one thing, managers often focus excessively on desired outcomes, without drilling down to the value drivers. They then run the risk of not achieving the desired outcomes.

McDonald's offers a vivid example of this principle—and everyone knows how successful McDonald's has been. Ray Kroc, who bought the franchise from the McDonald brothers, started not only a company but a whole industry. Although many people think of McDonald's as the leader in the franchising business, franchising itself was not a McDonald's innovation. Prior to McDonald's, however, franchisers focused on *selling* franchise licenses as the key value driver. The more licenses sold, the higher the revenue. Ray Kroc recognized that selling more franchise licenses was merely a desired outcome. The real value driver was what the franchiser could do to make the franchisee more successful and hence enhance the value of the license. McDonald's thus focused on franchisee training, simple menus with limited items to simplify restaurant management, and national advertising campaigns that benefited all franchisees. The correct recognition of the key value driver in the business was instrumental in the company's success.

The principle applies at the personal level, as well. For example, a few years ago I met a Marketing manager from a large consumer-products company—call him Joe. Joe had responsibility for marketing a particular group of products, and his bonus was based largely on the sales revenue generated by that product group. He had recently been promoted from a field sales position.

My initial conversation with Joe was about his frustration in his new job. Sales had been increasing on his watch, but he was having numerous arguments with the manager of the plant where the product was being manufactured. Most of these arguments were around stock keeping unit (SKU) complexity. Joe had introduced a few new variations in the products he was responsible for—some added features, new colors, and the like—that had helped boost sales. The plant manager complained that these features increased his manufacturing costs.

Joe couldn't understand why his boss, to whom the plant manager also reported, would not simply settle this dispute by emphasizing the importance of sales growth. And why wasn't his boss patting him on the back for his creativity in introducing new product variations?

About a year after this initial conversation, I ran into Joe again in connection with a consulting assignment with this company. He was transformed. Apparently, all his frustrations were behind him. He explained it as follows:

> I finally decided to look at things the way my boss did, rather than what seemed to be in my best interest. I realized that, as product group vice president, my boss was being compensated not only on sales but on how much Economic Value the product group generated. This meant he also cared about manufacturing costs and how much inventory was tied up in the value chain. My new product variations were pumping up sales, but they were also increasing manufacturing costs and inventory-carrying charges. I asked myself what I would do if I wanted to maximize my boss's bonus rather than my own.
>
> The answer was not necessarily to stop being innovative in creating new product variations. But I was now much more focused on minimizing the variety of components we were manufacturing or purchasing. Product variety now comes from creating more combinations from fewer components. Our overall component SKUs are down, but our sales growth hasn't slowed.

Joe's experience is a clear illustration of how the recognition of value drivers transforms decision making. The first step was for him to recognize that higher sales was a desired outcome, not a value driver. The real driver of value was having sufficient product variety to achieve a desired sales growth *without* increasing the variety or complexity of the component inventory. The second step was to understand how this value driver influenced the way his boss (one level above him in the organization) looked at the value chain. And finally, he personally introduced an innovation in the management of this key value driver. In a sense, Joe was successful only when he behaved like that secretary who wanted to understand what made me effective and valuable.

What Are All the Activities You and Your Organization Are Involved in to Create Value?

When I ask managers this question, I typically get answers that have to do with the products or services that their companies produce. I hear statements like: "We create value by making personal computers" or "We create value by making consumer durables."

These kinds of statements betray a lack of understanding of the question. Making a personal computer is the outcome of a set of value-creating activities, rather than a value-creating activity in itself. Indeed, if the value of a personal computer to the user was less than the direct and indirect (opportunity) costs of making it, its creation would destroy value. For example, the technology of making electric cars for road use is available today, but the price at which consumers would purchase such cars is less than what it would cost to make them. An organization set up to make and sell electric cars would not be creating value in today's environment. Instead, it would create cars but destroy value until production costs were lowered sufficiently below the value of such a car to consumers to allow it to be sold for a reasonable price.

The Importance of Knowing How You Create Value
The creation of any product or service involves a bundle of activities. Some of them may be adding value, some may be destroying value. It is important to know what each activity does in terms of value creation, both in the short term and the long term. Just because an organization is creating value as a whole doesn't mean that everything it does is creating value.

To see this, consider automobile companies. When Henry Ford started making cars, his company made everything from the tires to the engine in the car and its body. It made sense to be so vertically integrated because Ford could make just about anything that went into a car better than anybody else. Over time, however, companies began to specialize. There were tire manufacturers who could make better tires cheaper than Ford could. There were automobile component manufacturers who were better than Ford at making specific components such as axles and brakes. If Ford remained vertically integrated as it had been in the past, many of its activities would be destroying value because the direct and opportunity costs for Ford to make tires, axles, and brakes would exceed the prices at which Ford could buy them from external suppliers. As a result, Ford—like most car manufacturers today—outsources many of the components that go into making a car.

Two Levels of Understanding: Organizational and Personal
Every organization engages in a wide range of activities to create value—even though people's notions of value creation do not always serve the interests of the larger meaning of value to the organization as a whole. Moreover, although people often have a good idea of how their own functional area creates value, they commonly fail to appreciate how value is being created in other parts of the organization.

Consider, for example, a manufacturing company that prides itself on engineering excellence and a keen awareness of the bottom line, or the delivery of shareholder value. A few years ago, I was consulting with senior Finance executives in such an organization. We were discussing the implementation of a new resource allocation system, and much of the discussion was focused on technical finance and accounting issues. We also had a facilitator to help us, a Human Resources (HR) manager. At one point, the HR manager wanted us to break into groups to discuss the implementation of the new system in light of the organization's culture. One of the Finance executives spoke up and asked whether we could postpone that discussion since we still had so many technical issues to cover. The HR manager quietly withdrew her suggestion.

Immediately after this we took a short coffee break. As we were walking down the hallway, one of the colleagues of this Finance executive thanked him for "rescuing" the group from a breakout session on organizational culture. The executive turned and whispered, "We don't really have time for all that touchy-feely crap."

As it turned out, we did have a lot of technical issues to cover and barely enough time in which to do it. But the cultural requirements that were necessary for the success of the new process were never discussed. When the process was implemented, these requirements were not met, and the process never took hold in the organization the way we had hoped.

This story illustrates what happens in many organizations: people tend to overestimate the value created by the activities their own function or group or department engages in, and underestimate the value created by others (in this instance, the value created by HR). As a result they rarely look at their own area for opportunities to cut out unproductive activities or outsource, and they view resources being allocated to groups whose activities are very different from their own as value-dissipating. Understanding which organizational activities create value and how is an essential part of being an effective value creator. This is an issue of perspectives within the organization. There are usually multiple perspectives on value creation in any organization, and people from different parts of the organization are likely to have different and conflicting views about which activities create value.

There is a personal message here as well. Becoming a great value creator means reflecting on all that you do for the organization and asking yourself, What activities are creating value, in that I am doing them better than anyone else can? What activities are destroying value, in that someone else could do them better than I am? How does each of my activities relate to the bottom-line meaning of value for my organization? And what else could I do that would more effectively add to the value created by my organization?

Answering these questions can transform the way you look at your work and your job. For example, there is something that someone else can do better, find a way to eliminate it from the set of activities you perform. "Outsource" it!

People often resist outsourcing tasks because they are afraid that doing so will make them seem redundant to the organization. But the opposite is true: the more time you free up from the things you don't do very well or enjoy doing, the more time you will have to focus on the activities you excel at and the more valuable you will be to your organization in the long run. This is the economic principle that what counts is comparative advantage, not absolute advantage. A friend of mine who is a consultant described his discovery of this key point:

> I don't mow the lawn or prepare my tax returns any more. I have a CPA and an MBA with a concentration in finance. I can certainly do my taxes. And I'm pretty good at mowing the lawn too. But there are dedicated professionals out there who are better at those things than I am. And whose rates are lower than what I charge my clients per hour.

I used to do a lot of my own financial analysis for the consulting work I do. I don't do that anymore either. I have hired someone for the job. Where my time is best spent is on creating new products for my clients, helping them solve problems, and building client relationships. That's all I spend my time on now.

What Is Your Strategy?

A strategy is a road map for getting to a goal. Strategy determines how resources are allocated, both human and financial. It provides a mechanism by which an organization can examine all of its value-creating activities and decide which ones to focus on to reach its goal. Strategy is thus a way to achieve focus. Those who consistently create value know the enormous power of focus in maximizing effectiveness.

The Power of Strategy
One of the advantages of a clearly enunciated strategy is that it can help you cut out some activities—even if they are creating value—so as to concentrate more effectively on other activities that may better maximize value. In other words, *one of the important objectives of strategy is to say no to good ideas.* A good illustration of the power of strategy is the birth and explosive development of Starbucks, the global coffee powerhouse.

A Whole Different Cup: Starbucks

In 1987, the coffee industry in the United States was dominated by three major players, Procter & Gamble (P&G), General Foods, and Nestlé. Collectively these three giants accounted for 90 percent of the $8 billion retail market. By 1988, P&G was winning the market share battle with its Folgers brand, but profit margins were declining for all the major competitors, along with per-capita coffee consumption in the United States.

The major competitors shared the same strategy, which was to target the entire grocery-buying public and sell mass-produced ground coffee that was made with inexpensive Robusta beans and vacuum-packed for long shelf life. The key dimension on which the major producers competed was price. None of them was creating much value.

But in 1986, Howard Schultz had opened the first Starbucks café in Seattle. By the end of 1994, Starbucks was a publicly traded company worth over $1 billion. How did this happen?

Schultz had a very different strategy. First, instead of targeting the entire grocery-buying public, he focused on upwardly mobile white-collar workers familiar with the "European cappuccino culture." This meant avoiding grocery-store selling. Instead, Starbucks opened cafés that were close to its customers' places of work. Second, rather than competing on price, Starbucks decided to offer its customers the entire experience of having fine coffee in an inviting café atmosphere. This meant producing high-quality coffee with more expensive Arabica beans and selling the product at relatively high profit margins. Starbucks succeeded because it had a distinctive strategy that focused on a different set of value drivers, thus producing a quite different set of decisions from those of the major coffee producers. Its focus resulted in enormous value creation for Starbucks' shareholders.

Two Levels of Understanding: Organizational and Personal

Understanding your organization's strategy is important for being an effective value creator, no matter what your level in the organization. Too often people think strategy is the responsibility of senior management or perhaps just the CEO. It is true that those at the top ultimately decide the company's strategic direction. But influencing and executing strategy is everybody's business. The execution of strategy is all about allocating resources, including time and effort—something all employees control to some degree, certainly those in supervisory and managerial positions. And you can't execute the strategy unless you understand it.

One of the qualities I have observed in managers who consistently excel at value creation is that they have internalized their company's strategy to such an extent that its execution becomes instinctive. They don't have to think about it; it simply guides all their decisions. It's a bit like a player on a football team who understands the game plan so well that he can immediately react to any situation and make adjustments during a play that maximize its likelihood of success, without deviating from the basic structure of the game plan.

Understanding the organization's strategy is not enough, however. You must also have a personal strategy for success that allows you to excel while operating within the parameters set by the organizational strategy. Setting strategy at the personal level involves the same principles that apply to corporate strategy—but you are now the boss. The strategy is entirely your call.

Most people don't bother to consciously define their personal strategy. This means that they are not deliberate in the use of their personal resources—their time and effort. If you have a personal strategy, you will have a plan for

- What will you focus on professionally
- How will you grow personally
- What decisions will you make on a day-to-day basis that will be different as a result of your strategy

Like a sound organizational strategy, an effective personal strategy results in greater focus. It entails saying no to things that would dilute your value-creation efforts, such as tasks that could be performed more efficiently, at less cost, or with better quality by someone else. In other words, an effective personal strategy also focuses your attention on activities where you have the greatest comparative advantage.

How Do You and Your Organization Measure Success?

A strategy is an action plan for making progress toward a goal. But how do you know whether you're making progress? The only way to tell is to have a way to measure success.

How do you measure your personal success? Some people define success on the basis of the assessment their boss makes of their performance. Others have more internally driven measures of success. How you measure success is pivotal to how you behave.

Several years ago, I was consulting with a company whose HR group was a mix that included some highly energized leaders who understood their potential in driving organizational change and many others who were stuck in a traditional "staff support" mind-set. The vice president of HR, the most senior HR executive in the company, was one of those in the latter group. His objective seemed to be to avoid disturbing the status quo and to faithfully execute what he perceived as the will of the CEO, no questions asked.

I was once at a meeting that included the CEO, the vice president of HR, and an HR middle manager. As we discussed some difficult change issues the company was facing, I began to raise some uncomfortable questions about leadership, value creation, and change. For the most part, the CEO gave perceptive and candid answers, but some of his responses clearly conflicted with the way human resources were currently being managed in the firm. However, not once did the HR vice president dissent. In fact, his approach was to visibly agree with every statement made by the CEO, virtually repeating what the CEO had just said. To my surprise, it was the HR middle manager who dissented and challenged the CEO on a couple of occasions.

I remember thinking afterward about the striking contrast between the middle manager and the HR vice president. I wondered how both could survive in the same organization. But I also understood in that moment many of the inefficiencies that plagued this company—a stagnant and unduly complex compensation structure that was not linked effectively to value creation; leadership and succession planning that was not well understood by those most likely to be affected by it; loss of valuable employees at key junctures; and an HR group that was viewed by the rest of the organization as contributing to expenses and little else.

A few months after this incident, the middle manager resigned to accept a position with another company. The HR vice president unexpectedly resigned a few weeks later. There were rumors that he had been fired.

It is easy to see how each person in this case defined success. For the HR vice president, personal success was being "in the good books" of the CEO. For the HR middle manager, it was making constructive changes in the organization, even if it meant risking the boss's displeasure by apparently disagreeing with him.

Sunflower Management and Personal Success

For many people, pleasing the boss is a primary goal, not merely the desired outcome of meeting value creation objectives. People like that behave like sunflowers—they are constantly watching the boss for cues about how to behave, like sunflowers following the sun.[1]

Society has a derogatory term for such people. Whether male or female, they're called *yes-men.* Yet this apparent dismissal disguises a deeper truth. Yes-men exist because most bosses like them. They make the boss feel good and enhance the boss's ego. Ask yourself: who are the people I like most in my organization and how often do these people disagree with me?

Just as important, yes-men often appear to the organization to be "team players." They are willing to "go with the flow" and subordinate their personal views for "the greater good of the group." Most groups value team harmony and view dissent as a threat to this harmony. And organizations that emphasize the value of teamwork and harmony inadvertently send a message that being a yes-man is desirable.

But what are the risks and opportunity costs? Yes-men tend to produce at least four undesirable outcomes: they mislead, they are reactive instead of being proactive, they refuse to be creative and take risks, and they do not embrace change.

It was perhaps the fear of his group being infected with the yes-man disease that prompted Alfred P. Sloan Jr., to make the following statement: "Gentlemen, I take it we are all in complete agreement on the decision here. . . . Then I propose we postpone further discussion of this matter until our next meeting to give ourselves time to develop disagreements and perhaps gain some understanding of what the decision is all about."[2]

In the "dot-com" age, organizations cannot afford yes-men. Instead, they need people who are

- Proactive rather than reactive
- Creative
- Willing to speak their mind and take risks
- Aggressive enough to capture all the opportunities to create value

Such people have their own internal measures of success. And they understand that *success* can only mean creating genuine value for the organization. To understand where you can find such people, you need to first understand the process by which people become yes-men.

The Process of Becoming a Yes-Man
People are not born as yes-men. It is often the leaders in the organization who make employees into yes-men.

Imagine your boss calling you into her office and telling you about a great idea she has that the company might want to try. She asks you to investigate the idea and then give your opinion. Your boss, who not only owns the company but also controls your future with the company, is clearly excited about the idea.

Suppose you investigate the idea and discover it's a dog. What do you do?

It is obviously your moral responsibility to tell the truth. But what is the consequence? If you tell your boss it's a bad idea, there are two possibilities that your boss has to consider. One is that you are right and it is truly a bad idea. The other is that the idea is as good as she thought it was, but you are a lousy analyst who lacks the skill to do the kind of sophisticated analysis needed to discover that it's a good idea. It is difficult for your boss, no matter how rational, to separate these two possibilities in her mind. Thus, she will commingle the assessment of the idea with an assessment of your ability. Anticipating this, you may well decide to tell your boss what you think she wants to hear.

When the people in charge fall victim to the seductive appeal of yes-men—when, subtly or otherwise, they encourage employees to tell them what they want to hear—the entire organization suffers. Cynicism sets in as people begin to view the organization as a political place to play zero-sum games. Jack Welch aptly describes such an organization as one with "its face toward the CEO and its ass toward the customer."

Two Levels of Understanding: Organizational and Personal
Sunflower management is perhaps the most insidious enemy of authentic measures of success. The most important thing to remember about sunflower management is this: though it seems expedient in the short run, a person who is viewed as a yes-man is ultimately likely to be viewed as dispensable by the organization. In the long run, few people value individuals who are merely echoes of their own voice. An organization whose culture breeds yes-men will never be able to sustain value creation, because it will fail to take advantage of the breakthrough thinking that often results from the cacophony of diverse viewpoints that are expressed freely in organizations where people feel empowered to express themselves honestly.

In any organization that is itself poised to create significant value, those who tell the truth will be recognized and rewarded in the long run. If you become convinced that your organization is not one of those, find a way to leave. Your organization is going nowhere, and you are going with it!

Being honest does not mean being abrasive and unpleasant. The most effective value creators I have seen disagree with charm, and with a smile. They express their opinions without seeming confrontational. They have tact and people skills. They realize that a disagreement is always loaded with the potential to be viewed as an act of hostility, and make a conscious effort to defuse that potential by the *way* they disagree.

The point, of course, is not only to speak the truth but to speak it in a way that will be useful. Effective value creators dare to disagree because they are focused on real issues of value creation and destruction. That is, they understand the organization's mission. They know what real value means in the context of their organization. They understand the organization's strategy. They have taken inventory of the activities that create value. They understand the conflicting perspectives within an organization that can impede genuine value creation. And they use these assessments as their barometers of organizational and personal success.

As you come to a clearer understanding of these points, you will be able to measure your own success in more meaningful terms—not by how much you please your superiors in the short term, but by the positive impact you have on value creation in your organization.

How Fast Are You at Creating Value?

Speed is one of the enabling attributes of an effective value creator. It doesn't matter whether you're talking about an individual or an organization. The importance of speed is the same. As Tom Peters writes, "It's real simple. If we're not getting more, better, faster than they are getting more, better, faster, then we're getting less better or more worse faster than they are."

Speed and Quality
People often confuse speed with lack of quality. After all, if it's done really fast, quality must have been compromised. There are, of course, abundant examples of sloppily done things that were done fast. But that is not the kind of speed I'm talking about. Speed is meaningless unless combined with high quality.

My favorite organizational example of speed is the world record for the shortest time to build a house from scratch: less than three hours, breaking the previous record of four hours. A group in San Diego, California, did everything from digging the foundation to completing the landscaping. Not only was the house built in eye-popping time, it met all the stringent San Diego city building code standards, and did not cost any more than the usual house of its size.[3]

Thus speed does not have to sacrifice quality—if it does, then it's not genuine speed. It does not contribute to value creation but destroys it instead. The point is that both organizations and individuals can achieve quantum leaps in speed only if they make doing so a priority and devote energy and creativity to the task.

The notion that speed is an essential aspect of value creation can redefine a whole corporate culture. For example, in 1999 Federated Department Stores, the $17 billion retail giant, appointed a man named Love Goel as the CEO of its e-commerce division. Goel was twenty-eight years old and had come to the United States from India a mere seven years earlier. This is how Love Goel describes his quest: "We have people here who think growth is 3 percent a year. But we're growing 500 percent this year. People know how to do things. But they know how to do it in six months. I want them to do it in six days."[4]

Two Levels of Understanding: Organizational and Personal
At the organizational level, becoming faster requires a fundamental cultural change. As a whole, the organization must become more tolerant of mistakes. Faster decisions often mean decisions made with less information. This, in turn, typically

□

means a greater likelihood of errors. One of the reasons why decision making in some organizations is slow is that individuals perceive a high personal cost to making mistakes. Hiding behind organizational processes, even if they slow you down, is often much safer than making fast decisions. For its part, the organization prefers elaborate processes for making decisions because they provide a uniform framework for decisions and help to diminish errors and chaos.

This implies that to speed up decision making, the first step an organization needs to take is to change the processes by which decisions are made and resources are allocated. These processes must emphasize speed over accuracy. The second step is to change the organizational culture. It must become more forgiving of individual errors, particularly those that result from attempts to improve creativity and speed. It's a bit like basketball. As a coach, you may want to punish a player who makes mistakes as a result of inattentiveness or laziness. But you want to encourage a player who takes a really good shot and misses or commits an inadvertent foul while playing good, aggressive defense. Addressing these two organizational issues will resolve 85–90 percent of the problems that slow the organization down.

At the individual level, the challenge is to emphasize speed and quality as part of your personal value system. Always seek ways to improve your personal speed. Learn to derive joy from it. This is basically mental conditioning. The more you enjoy speed, the more speed will befriend you.

■ Value Creation Is a Journey

Good value creators know that effective value creation is a journey, not a destination. It is a process of constant evolution. Success is always measured relative to internally created goals and yardsticks. The motivation comes from within, not outside.

This is why all five dimensions of value creation—the meaning of value, the activities being pursued to create value, the personal value creation strategy, the measures of success, and the speed of achievement—are in a state of flux and evolution for effective value creators. Every success leads to loftier goals. Every failure leads to a reexamination of the strategy to see if it needs to be recalibrated. But the goals are never lowered.

A few years ago I had the opportunity to ask a distinguished finance professor at a leading business school about his amazing productivity in research, teaching and service to the profession. This is what he said.

> You know, I thought I was doing as much as was humanly possible three years ago. There was no way I could do more. In fact, my wife was urging me to cut back, and I was beginning to seriously think about giving up some of the things I was doing. The problem was I enjoyed almost everything I was doing a bit too much.
>
> Today I'm doing twice as much as I was doing three years ago and spending more time with my family. I've given up a few things that I wasn't enjoying very much but was doing out of a sense of obligation. But that's been replaced by a lot more of things I truly enjoy. The funny thing is that the more you do, the better you get at doing more, and the better you get at doing more, the more you do. It's a never-ending loop.

CHAPTER SUMMARY

Creating value is the central purpose of both organizations and individuals. For profit-making organizations, value can be defined as Economic Value, which is roughly interchangeable with shareholder value in the case of publicly traded corporations. A corresponding formulation defines what creating value means for individuals within the organization. Simply put, organizations and individuals succeed to the extent that they engage in sustained value creation.

The five keys to being a great value creator involve having (1) a clear definition of the meaning of value for a specific organization, (2) a clear understanding of the activities that create value and the multiple perspectives on value creation that exist in the organization, (3) a clear understanding of strategy, (4) an appropriate measure of success, and (5) a mastery of speed without sacrificing quality. Organizations who master these keys can achieve sustained value creation; individuals that master them become more valuable to their organization and in the marketplace.

Creating value is a never-ending process of reinventing oneself, one's job, and the organization. In the next chapter, I will explore the first two keys to value creation in depth. You will see how the meaning of value in an organization is defined, the factors that can prevent a common understanding of value within the organization, and the sources of multiple perspectives on the activities that create value—perspectives that can enhance or impede the value-creation efforts of both the organization and the individuals within it.

Reflections and Discussion

Organizational Steps for Value Creation
1. How does your organization define *value?* Write down as many definitions of value as you believe are current in your organization.
2. From your list in item 1, pick the definition that you believe is most important to your organization's success. How widely shared is the conviction in your organization that this is how value should be defined?
3. List the key activities your organization or functional area engages in. Which of these are creating value in the sense that your organization is better at them than any other organization? Which activities could be done better or less expensively outside the organization? Is this strictly the criterion the organization uses to determine what to outsource?
4. Write a brief paragraph describing your organization's strategy. How well is this strategy understood and internalized by everybody in your organization?
5. How is success measured in your organization or functional area? What does your organization do, if anything, to discourage sunflower management and support candid examinations of what creates and destroys value?

6. If you are a senior executive who is leading a part or all of your organization, ask yourself the following questions: (a) Are you working harder than anyone else in your organization? (b) Do you feel that you do more creative thinking than anyone else in your organization? and (c) Do you feel that no one else cares about the organization as much as you do?

   If the answers to these questions are all in the affirmative, you are probably surrounded by too many yes-men. Your first priority should be to examine how you might be encouraging sunflower management and create an action plan to eliminate it.

7. How much discomfort does the following statement by the CFO of an Internet company cause you? "If it takes you four days to make a major decision in a major corporation, you're doing well. If it takes you four days to make a major decision in an Internet company, you are a dead Internet company."

Personal Steps for Value Creation

1. What is your personal definition of value in the context of your job? How consistent is your definition with (a) how your organization defines value creation? (b) how your organization sees your value contribution?

2. List the ten most important activities (in terms of value creation) that you engage in. Put them in four categories: (a) those that you are uniquely equipped to perform (you are better at these than anyone else); (b) those that you are excellent at (there may be a few others who are as good as you at these, but you are in the top group of performers); (c) those that you are good at (these activities are above the threshold for acceptable performance but there are others who could do them better); and (d) those that you are below average at (your performance in these is below the threshold acceptable to you).

   Activities in (a) are part of your "organizational soul." Make sure that you invest most of your time and energy in these activities.

   You should strive to do as many of the activities in (b) as possible, but it is not a disaster if other commitments sometimes prevent you from performing these tasks. You can occasionally delegate them to those who can do them almost as well as you. Moreover, you should actively seek to develop "understudies," people who can step in for you to perform these tasks when you are tied up with more pressing matters.

Seek to actively delegate activities in (c). People who can do these activities as well as you or better already exist, so you do not have a developmental burden here. There is no harm in performing these tasks on an emergency basis when others are not available, but your goal should be to exclude them from your regular portfolio of activities.

Finally, delegate to others the activities in (d) at the first opportunity. Spending time on these is destroying personal value for you.

3. Write a brief paragraph describing your personal strategy for success. Then answer the following questions: (a) Will this strategy produce long-term value as I define it? (b) Does this strategy focus most of my time and energy on the activities I am unique and excellent at? (c) How does this strategy distinguish me from those around me?

4. How do you personally measure success? What is the relationship between your measure and your definition of what constitutes value in your organization?

5. To what extent does the way you measure success reflect sunflower management? Do you sometimes act like a yes-man in order to succeed?

6. How fast are you? Are you ever amazed at how much you are able to accomplish in so little time and with so much quality? Do you set goals that others would consider impossible? Are you having fun doing this? Or do you feel that you need to find ways to significantly increase your speed?

Understanding Value and Value Creation

The first chapter introduced the five secrets that great value creators master. This chapter and the next examine specific strategies for excelling at each of these five aspects of value creation. Both organizational and personal strategies are presented so that you can use the secrets of value creation to enhance your organization's success—and your own.

This chapter focuses on strategies related to the first two principles, understanding the meaning of value and understanding multiple perspectives on the activities that create value. These fundamental aspects of value creation have to do with how value is defined and understood at both the organizational and personal levels. Creating a shared and nuanced understanding of value, and of the activities that create value, is perhaps the most crucial step in harnessing energy to the core mission of an organization.

■ Defining Value and Focusing on Value Creation

Creating value is the core mission of any organization or individual. Yet it is clear that sustained value creation does not happen consistently. Ron Miller of the Walt Disney Company lost his job as CEO in 1984 despite the company's outstanding brand quality and Miller's family ties to Walt Disney himself. Al Dunlap, a one-time darling of Wall Street, was removed as CEO of Sunbeam Corporation in 1998. IBM fired John Akers as CEO in 1993 and replaced him with Lou Gerstner, despite the fact that the company was still a dominant force in the computer industry. In every case, the reason was the same: inability to sustain shareholder value creation, which is the bottom-line meaning of value for publicly held companies.

Sustained value creation requires, first of all, a tight focus on creating value. But even well-intentioned efforts will go astray unless a clear and accurate understanding of what constitutes value for a particular organization pervades the entire firm.

There are four main impediments to maintaining this univocal understanding of value. They are summarized in Figure 2.1. I'll review each of these impediments and then examine organizational and personal tools for overcoming them.

Lack of a Single Clear Definition of
Value and Understanding of Value Drivers

Many organizations haven't yet defined what value creation means to them. Or they have so many definitions of value—many of which conflict in specific circumstances—that employees end up being confused about the core mission of the company.

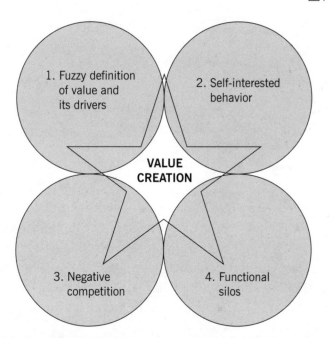

Figure 2.1. Four Main Impediments to a Clear Understanding of Value

As noted in Chapter One, in a for-profit organization, "value" simply means *Economic Value*, defined as

Economic Value = After-tax profit
– Opportunity cost of using capital

When Economic Value is created in a publicly owned company, so is shareholder value. The reason is that the opportunity cost of using capital includes the cost incurred by the shareholders in giving the organization the use of their capital. So what is left over is truly the economic surplus generated by the organization for its owners, the shareholders.

To see an example of Economic Value, suppose your company has an income statement that looks like this in a given year (indicated in parentheses are the stakeholders who affect that item significantly):

Sales (*Customers, Employees*)	$100
– Cost of Goods Sold (*Employees, Suppliers*)	$50
– Sales, General & Administrative Expenses (*Employees, Customers*)	$20
Operating Profit	$30

If your effective tax rate is 40 percent, then your after-tax operating profit (before financing charges like debt interest) is $30 \times (1 - 0.4) = \$18$. Now suppose you have $150 in assets on your balance sheet and the weighted average of the opportunity costs of your debt and equity financing is 10 percent. Then the Economic Value generated by your company this year is

$$\$18 - 0.10 \times \$150 = \$3$$

If Economic Value is positive, as it is here, your company has created value in that year. If it is negative, your company has destroyed value. The goal of any for-profit organization should be to sustain the creation of a positive and growing Economic Value over time.

Although this concept is straightforward, many organizations lack a clear definition of what sustained value creation means to them. In fact, there is often a debate in public corporations about whether shareholder value is even the appropriate definition of value. After all, any organization has multiple stakeholders—customers, employees, and suppliers, for example—so why are shareholders at the top of the value pyramid?

There are two simple reasons why "shareholder value" is the preferred measure of value. First, the measure of shareholder value is Economic Value, and Economic Value creation cannot be sustained unless the organization is also creating value for all its other stakeholders. This is true for publicly as well as privately held companies. To see this, go back to the example of the company that generated $3 in Economic Value in a particular year. If the company is not keeping its customers happy with the products they want, it will not be able to sustain sales growth. Similarly, it takes committed and creative employees to grow sales, even if you have good products. So, the top line in the income statement—the money coming in—will be compromised if two important stakeholders, customers and employees, are dissatisfied.

The same point applies to costs. Suppliers, for example, have a major impact on what it costs you to produce what you sell. Having committed employees who develop good relationships with suppliers is an important driver of these costs. By the same token, your brand equity with your customers determines how much you need to spend on advertising and other marketing activities to generate the desired sales revenue. Controlling costs, and thus improving the bottom line, then involves the interests of multiple stakeholders. The point is simply this—to create *sustained* shareholder value, you must also make all your other stakeholders happy. By stating a single comprehensive goal as that of maximizing shareholder value, you subsume all the other possible goals you could have.

By way of analogy, imagine a village in which there is one hunter who goes out and kills deer for the whole village. He promises to eat only after everyone else has had enough to eat. In this case, if the village states its goal as making sure that the deer hunter never goes hungry, then it will automatically have to make sure that there is enough deer to feed everybody in the village. While achieving the goal may occasionally call for sacrifices by some villagers who eat a bit less to leave some food for the hunter, in the long run the village will focus on activities that ensure that enough deer will be killed to feed everybody. Maintaining this focus will involve decisions like locating the village near water where deer drink, providing the hunter with enough resources (including helpers), and so on.

Like the deer hunter, shareholders are the last to eat, and thus it is the goal of maximizing their welfare that should drive the organization. Employees, like the villagers, may occasionally have to make sacrifices to accommodate the shareholders. But in the long run, the interests of all stakeholders must be accounted for if the shareholders are to be happy.

The second reason to maximize shareholder value is that shareholders have the highest *control rights* vested in them, as is reflected in the power to remove the CEO. Why should shareholders have these rights?

Think again of the deer hunter. The right thing for the village to do would be to allow the deer hunter to name the village chief, who in turn decides where to locate the village, how many people will assist the hunter, and how many people to train to clean the deer and cook it. All of these decisions should be made to maximize the likelihood that the deer hunter will have more than enough to eat. Since the deer hunter is the last to eat, focusing decisions in this way will maximize the welfare of the entire village.

Like the deer hunter, shareholders have the lowest-priority *financial claim* on the firm's cash flows. You first pay off your suppliers, your employees, your bondholders, your bank and even the government before you pay the shareholders a penny. So the only efficient way to structure the corporation is to give shareholders the greatest control rights. More generally, any efficiently designed corporation must create an inverse relationship between the priority of a financial claim and the control rights vested in that claim, as shown in Figure 2.2.

As financial claim priority goes up, control rights go down. Suppliers and vendors have the least control over what the corporation does. Employees have more control, but if the firm's performance fails to satisfy certain conditions, the creditors can

Figure 2.2. Financial Claim Priority and Control Rights

step in and tell the employees what to do. Shareholders have a lower financial claim priority than creditors, but can dictate to the employees in virtually any circumstance, not just when the firm's performance fails to meet specified criteria.

To summarize, the two reasons for making shareholder value your overarching definition of value are first that shareholders have the lowest-priority financial claim, so attending to their welfare will also help address the concerns of all stakeholders in the long run, and second that shareholders have the highest control rights.

I cannot overemphasize the importance of having a single clear definition of value that everyone in the organization understands. Too often there are so many different notions of value and so many different performance metrics that few employees understand what they are really supposed to do. One manager expressed his frustration to me:

> Our company is run by an alphabet soup. We have EPS, ROE, RONA, ROI, Operating Profit, Customer Satisfaction Scores, Employee Satisfaction Scores, Stock Price, IRR, NPV and payback, all affecting how we make decisions. At the end of the day I sometimes feel like screaming: "What do you really want me to do here?" I don't think I'm the only one who's confused.

The antidote to this situation is to have a single, clear, and shared definition of value. This does not mean that there is only one way to *create* value. The next section will explore the many activities that contribute to value creation as well as the multiple perspectives on value that exist in any organization. But organizations and individuals alike must tie their perspectives on value creation and their gauges of performance to the true (often multidimensional) meaning of value in the organization.

Organizational Strategy for Clear Definition of Value
There are four simple steps to addressing the problem from an organizational standpoint:

1. Choose a clear definition of value for your organization that is focused on maximizing shareholder value. (Economic Value is an example; there are others as well.)
2. Make sure everyone in the organization understands that the goal is to maximize that value over the *long run*. There must be people dedicated to the task of understanding what value means and teaching others about it.
3. Educate all your employees about the value drivers they can manage to maximize value. Which are the value drivers under their control and how can they manage them better?
4. Tie compensation directly to value creation or to the value drivers employees can control. Preaching about value maximization while tying compensation to factors that employees don't see as being highly correlated with that notion of value is a recipe for disaster.

Personal Strategy for Clear Definition of Value
At a personal level, you need to be clear about value as well. If you are not, it's often too easy to get distracted by activities that dilute your focus on value creation. As you proceed through this book, you should develop an increasingly clear concept of value.

As you do, take the following steps:

1. *Determine your own personal definition of value creation and decide how maximizing this value differs from maximizing your immediate compensation.* In an ideal world, there would be no difference between these two. But in practice, there often is. What do you want to maximize?
2. *Identify the activities you are currently engaged in that do not maximize your value creation potential.* Develop an action plan to minimize or phase out these activities over the next twelve months.
3. *Make it a goal to achieve at least three significant things each year that do not directly affect your own compensation but enhance the performance of others, including your boss.* Recall the example of my secretary: by contributing to the performance of the professors, she simultaneously created value for the department and enhanced her own.

Self-Interested Behavior That Conflicts with Value Creation

A few years ago, I was talking to a friend who had been given a large consulting contract with a major company. He was scheduled to begin working on the project in March of the following year. He told me that he had received a call in late November from a Human Resources executive who wanted to know if my friend would mind receiving his entire consulting fee for next year's services sometime during December *this* year.

Apparently, the reason for this remarkable generosity was that the HR executive had a surplus in the expense budget for the current year. If this money was not spent, there was no guarantee it would be around next year. So this executive was willing to impose the tangible opportunity cost on the organization of paying a consultant almost a year in advance of when he would normally be paid.

Imposing a cost on the organization just to "spend the budget" is only one example of self-interested behavior by individuals in organizations. By *self-interested behavior,* I simply mean those actions that are either in individuals' narrow self-interest or in the parochial interest of the group they belong to but that diminish value creation for the organization as a whole. Such behavior is all too common in organizations. And the larger the organization, the worse the potential problem.

People don't engage in such behavior when it's their own business they are running. One of the hardest things in any organization with separation of ownership and management is to make employees feel and behave like owners. One manager told me that he always explained to the employees that the company was like a house, and that he wanted them to act like they were owners, not rent-paying tenants.

Organizational Strategy for Discouraging
Self-Interested Behavior by Employees
The propensity to engage in self-interested behavior may be the most important characteristic that distinguishes humans from machines. There is little hope of eliminating it altogether, but there are steps that organizations can take to minimize it.

1. *Pay the employees the way owners get paid.* That means
   - Paying employees based on performance rather than duration on the job
   - Linking compensation to shareholder value and the drivers of shareholder value
   - Not imposing any upper bounds on what value creators can earn, so that if an employee creates $1 of additional value for the organization, that employee should get a fraction of that, with no upper bound on total compensation
   - Making employees bear the risk of negative bonuses if their performance destroys value—or firing employees who destroy value if negative bonuses are not feasible

2. *Facilitate true empowerment.* The word *empowerment* is often misunderstood. It does not mean giving someone more power. You are never empowered if someone gives you power. True empowerment comes from within. Think of the source of empowerment for Mahatma Gandhi, Jesus Christ, Martin Luther King, and others who transformed entire societies. However, the organization can facilitate employee empowerment by

   - Creating more rewarding jobs in which employees truly enjoy what they are doing
   - Giving employees more real decision-making authority and accountability rather than just more work
   - Making sure that employees understand that their tasks have consequences for measurable outcomes that matter to the organization
   - Building trust—that is, convincing employees that they will not be hurt if they act in an empowered way

3. *Lead by example.* If an organization wants its employees to avoid acting in their narrow self-interest at the expense of the organization, then its leaders must behave that way too. That means "walking the talk." Nothing corrodes an organization's culture faster than senior leaders who preach the importance of shareholder value and organizational success and then pursue their own selfish interests at the expense of shareholder value. Such selfishness may manifest itself in executive compensation or expensive and highly visible perquisites.

To be sure, these steps are easier said than done. But they are essential for having empowered employees. In particular, building trust requires a tolerance for honest mistakes, an organizational culture that truly rewards risk taking rather than just paying lip service to it, and open sharing of information rather than treating information as a strategic weapon and a source of power.

Personal Strategy for Overcoming Self-Interested Behavior
Deciding to subjugate your own narrow self-interest to the
larger good of the organization is not easy. Often it is not in your
short-term interest, either, but it is nonetheless essential. Sometimes this is difficult because people are not clear about what
their priorities should be and how they can attend to the larger
good of the organization. Here's how one senior executive explained how he approached educating an employee about the
true responsibilities of the job:

> We had just hired an MBA who was appointed my executive
> assistant. His exact title was something else, but executive as-
> sistant is the best way to describe what he was supposed to do.
> At our first meeting, he asked me what my expectations of him
> were. I told him it was real simple. His job was to do whatever
> it took to make *me* more effective. I explained that this implied
> that rather than my trying to describe to him what his job was,
> he should try and understand what my job was. We spent a
> couple of hours going over all that I did, and then I asked him
> to spend the next two weeks just observing everything I did. I
> gave him no specific assignments those two weeks. But he was
> everywhere I was.

Obviously, this is not the only way to get clarity about your
job. The point is that it may be a good idea to involve your boss
in determining your top priorities.

Here are some steps that can help you focus your attention
on the good of the organization:

1. *Understand clearly (a) what you are getting paid for and (b) what
   you will need to do to get promoted.*
   - Pick the top two activities from each of these two areas,
     write them on a piece of paper, and paste the paper on
     your desk. This will remind you about the four most im-
     portant things you need to do to succeed in your job as
     it is defined for you.

- Talk with your boss to get clarity on this point, because it's not as simple as it sounds.

2. *Add two more items to your list that are not part of the job description but that would (a) make your job more enjoyable for you, and (b) add real value to the organization.* Understand that you are probably not going to be rewarded by the organization for doing these things, at least in the short run. But the long-run payoff to you could be spectacular.

3. *Add two more items to your list: (a) a specific set of actions that you will pursue consistently to empower yourself, and (b) a specific thing you will do to help those around you, especially those who report to you, to become more empowered.*

When you are done, you should have eight items on your list. At the end of every week, grade yourself on how well you did on each of these eight items and what you can do to improve. Assess your *personal value added* (PVA) to the organization as follows:

PVA = Quantification of dollar benefits produced
for the organization by my activities
– My wages
– Opportunity cost of the assets I tied up with my activities

Your goal should be to increase your PVA each year by 20 percent or more. Of course, quantifying the benefits of all you do can be challenging—it's difficult to pin a dollar amount to the value of facilitating empowerment, for example. But it is a useful exercise nonetheless. You can always come up with an estimate of the benefits; it's just that in some cases the estimates may be very imprecise.

The Negative Zone of Competition

It is well accepted that competition inspires people and organizations to scale great heights. Microsoft is famous for its rallying battle slogans. There are countless other examples. More tangibly, many executive compensation plans are structured to motivate employees by the desire to beat the competition and sometimes even to outdo others within the same organization. In economics, there is a whole literature on how senior executives can structure "tournaments" within their own organizations, so that employees are motivated to elevate their productivity out of a desire to win the tournament.

Stoking employees' competitive fires will be effective most of the time when the entire organization works in unison to compete against other firms in the market. But it is not always possible to coordinate competition effectively. Once competitive fires have been lit, it is easy for them to spread *within* the organization—so that employees begin to compete with each other. This internal competition sometimes takes the form of employees within the same functional area competing for advancement. Sometimes it takes the form of different functional groups within the organization competing with each other. While such competition can be helpful up to a point, it can destroy value when this behavior is taken too far. When this happens, the organization has reached the "negative zone of competition."

An example will illustrate the point. I once had the opportunity to talk to a logistics manager whose request to buy a fleet of trucks had been turned down because he had exhausted his capital budget for the year. He then proceeded to *lease* these trucks. I asked him if he had done a lease-versus-buy analysis before he leased the trucks. He said no. He added somewhat facetiously that he'd read somewhere that God invented leasing as a way to get around capital budgeting constraints!

I asked this manager why it was so important to have those trucks. Couldn't the logistics function served by the trucks be outsourced? Did he know whether leasing the trucks was better than outsourcing? He said he honestly did not know. Moreover, he did not seem to care. Here is what he said:

What you have to understand is that in our company your organizational clout is determined by the assets you control. No group has shrunk itself to power and greatness in this company. We're all competing for a limited pool of resources. I would not be a very good manager for my group if I did not use all the means at my disposal to acquire all the resources my group needs.

This manager's views typify an attitude shared by many. They view resource allocation within the company as a tournament in which every group competes with other groups for resources. The issue of whether the resources being allocated to the group will create more value for the organization than if they were allocated to another group is of secondary importance. What is of primary importance is that the manager's own group gets the resources it wants.

Such behavior clouds people's thinking about value creation. It diverts an individual's focus from being a value creator to being politically successful in completing transactions within the organization. In the case of the logistics manager, for example, it turned out that outsourcing would have been a much better choice for the company than leasing trucks. But he did not see things this way because he was in the negative zone of competition.

Why, then, do people enter the negative zone of competition? There are two main reasons:

1. A greater allocation of resources to the group means more power for the group.
2. From the standpoint of the group, it is easy to believe that the resources being requested will actually generate additional value for the organization.

Despite the negative consequences, the reasoning that powers the negative zone of competition makes a great deal of practical sense, and that makes it very difficult to confront on a day-to-day basis. It's worth looking at in detail here so as to see where its long-term weaknesses lie.

The first reason seems intuitively obvious—anybody with organizational experience knows that the groups that are allocated the most resources are those with the most power. After all, the amount of senior executive attention that is devoted to a particular group depends, as it should, on the importance of that group to the overall success of the organization. Generally, the larger the group in terms of the resources it controls, the greater the role it will play in determining overall organizational success. Thus groups that control larger resource bases receive greater attention from senior management. As a result the people within those groups become more visible in the organization, and future organizational leaders are more likely to be drawn from those groups as well.

In addition, the *incremental* resources that are allocated to a particular group often depend on the resources the group already controls. For example, consider two manufacturing divisions in a typical large company. Division A has $100 million in property, plant, and equipment, while Division B has $50 million. Suppose each division has annual depreciation roughly equal to 10 percent of its invested capital base. Division A thus has an annual depreciation expense of $10 million, while Division B has an annual expense of $5 million. If the company has decided to continue with both divisions, Division A will typically be allocated more *new* capital every year than Division B. The reason is that the annual depreciation expense of each division will work as the starting point for determining capital allocation. Reinvesting an amount equal to depreciation is often considered the bare minimum to keep the business alive.

The division that receives the greater share of incremental resources can obviously tackle a larger number of new initiatives, everything else being equal. This means more opportunities to excel and be noticed for those who work in that division. There is consequently often a greater sense of excitement, growth, and future possibilities there than in the asset-poor division.

In addition to the relationship between resources and opportunities, people often enter the negative zone of competition because they genuinely believe that their initiatives truly enhance value for the organization. The problem is that the two reasons for seeking more resources—greater power and greater value creation—often interact. This means that the negative zone of competition can corrupt the logic by which members of a group conclude that a resource-consuming initiative will add true value. That is, they recognize that there are benefits to the group from obtaining more resources. So whenever assumptions have to be made to analyze the value-creation potential of an initiative, the choice of assumption is skewed in favor of the one that is likely to lead to a favorable assessment of the initiative. This problem is likely to be compounded by what psychologists call *groupthink,* or the lack of dissension in group decision making. Groupthink often results in groups' reaching consensus too quickly and making poor decisions because key assumptions are not sufficiently challenged by group members.

The negative zone of competition means that the actions of different functional groups within an organization will not necessarily be aligned with the interests or strategy of the organization as a whole. Fortunately, there are some effective ways to combat this problem.

Organizational Strategies for
Avoiding the Negative Zone of Competition
Like other forms of self-interested behavior, the negative zone of competition is difficult to root out completely. However, it can be diminished in two main ways:

1. *Rewarding people for adding organizational value rather than amassing more resources.* To see if you are doing this, ask yourself:
    -   Do we reward employees for underspending their budget or do we implicitly punish them?
    -   Do we reward groups for decreasing their use of resources when they can demonstrate that doing so will add more value?
    -   Do we have a process to seek out and highlight each year competitive activities within the organization that destroy value, and then an action plan to remedy the situation?
2. *Explicitly reward cross-functional collaboration by basing bonuses and other rewards on the success of cross-functional teams rather than just on individual performance.* This can help focus people's efforts on value to the whole organization rather than on the narrow interests of their own group.

*Personal Strategies for Avoiding
the Negative Zone of Competition*

There are two key steps you can take to minimize your likelihood of being personally trapped in the negative zone of competition.

1. *Seek value-maximizing solutions rather than those that maximize resources for your group.* Recognize that this strategy may make you unpopular with your group in the short run. You will probably need to help those around you appreciate that cooperation is usually better than competition.
2. *Publicize the initiatives you take under Step 1.* This apparent self-promotion has two advantages:
    -   It helps to minimize the danger that your actions will be misinterpreted by others as a sign of weakness or ineffectiveness.
    -   It sends a powerful message to others about the importance of value creation and may influence their behavior in a positive way.

By contributing to a refocusing of others' efforts, you will help produce the incentives for entering into the negative zone of competition. As a result, you will find it easier to continue acting in a way that maximizes value.

The Functional Silo Mentality

Sometimes the focus on value creation can be diluted by a natural propensity to develop a functional silo mentality. This means that how people visualize value creation is driven by what their group does, and they tend to lose sight of the spillover effects of this on value creation for the organization as a whole.

The importance of an organizational perspective rather than a functional perspective can be seen in the case of Quaker Oats prior to its adoption of Economic Value as a performance metric.[1]

Destroying Value by Mutual Agreement: Quaker Oats

As in many other companies, each functional group at Quaker Oats was evaluated on the basis of the part of the value chain that the function affected the most. Thus, Procurement was judged on the basis of the per-unit purchase cost of input materials, Manufacturing was judged on the basis of per-unit manufacturing cost, and Sales and Distribution was judged on the basis of on-time product availability.

How do you minimize per-unit purchase cost? By buying large quantities of inputs, of course. So Procurement availed itself of quantity discounts from suppliers and stocked up on massive amounts of raw materials. This suited Manufacturing fine, since it could take advantage of economies of scale in production and lower its per-unit production cost by churning out large quantities of Gatorade, Rice-A-Roni, and other products. The result was that the company filled its warehouses with plentiful supplies of an assortment of finished goods. The people in Sales and Distribution were delighted because this large inventory made it easy for them to provide on-time delivery of products to dealers.

So each functional group viewed value creation in a way that made their actions entirely consistent with each other. But did anybody really understand true value creation?

Because of the large quantities of finished goods inventories that Quaker Oats was piling up, converting these inventories into sales and hence into cash was a challenge. At the end of every quarter, large amounts of unsold inventory had to be liquidated. But the market could only absorb a smaller supply at the prices at which Quaker Oats normally sold its products, so the company had to engage in "trade loading" to sell off its inventory at the end of the quarter. *Trade loading* refers to the practice of giving volume discounts and reducing prices as part of sales campaigns in an effort to dispose of unsold goods. The idea is to hit the quarterly sales volume targets.

Unfortunately, because of the significant price concessions, this practice does not always create value for shareholders. In fact, in the case of Quaker Oats, this management approach was destroying value for two reasons. First, the large quantities of inventories being accumulated at various stages of the production process—raw materials, work in progress, and finished goods—led to a large asset base and lowered asset productivity. That is, the company was overcapitalized. This generated a high capital charge and lowered the net Economic Value for the company, leading to value destruction in every period. Second, the relatively low prices at which goods were dumped on the market at the end of the period led to an after-tax profit that was too low to create value, given the investment involved. This too lowered Economic Value.

The Quaker Oats case is a clear illustration of how different functional areas can "suboptimize" for the company as a whole because their definition of value is obscured by functional silos. At Quaker Oats, the cause of this mentality was in part the performance metrics the company was using. These performance metrics were customized for each group in a way that seemed to make sense, but that actually created functional silos that stood in the way of a comprehensive picture of value. The problem was not just that the activities in the different functional areas added value in different ways; in this case the activities that individually seemed to be creating value were, taken together, actually destroying it. This problem was resolved at Quaker Oats only after William Smithburg became CEO and changed its performance metrics to account for the use of capital.

Organizational Strategies for Avoiding
the Functional Silo Mentality
The problem of functional silos is so pervasive that many organizations have developed approaches to deal with it. Here are some that work well:

1. *Adopt performance metrics for employee compensation that cut across functional lines and attend to the entire value chain.* Economic Value is a good metric in this regard.
2. *Reward employees for identifying activities that could be performed more efficiently outside their own function.* Many activities could be performed more efficiently elsewhere in the organization or outside the organization through outsourcing. As with combating the negative zone of competition, this strategy requires a deliberate effort to counteract the natural tendencies within an organization to hoard power and resources.

Personal Strategies for Avoiding
the Functional Silo Mentality
At the personal level, there are several specific steps you can take to expand your mental horizon of value creation:

1. *Improve your understanding of multiple value-creation perspectives within your organization.* Look at perspectives that transcend your function. (The next section will present some tools to help you do this.)
2. *Ask for job rotations that give you experience in a variety of functional areas.*

3. *Develop friendships with people who work in different functional areas.*

4. *Seek opportunities to work on projects that will put you on teams that include employees from other functional areas or in other geographical regions.*

5. *Seek opportunities to work on projects that are outside of your area of expertise and take you out of your comfort zone.*

■ Understanding Multiple Value-Creation Perspectives

Different functional units within an organization often work at cross-purposes because they have different perspectives about *how* value is created. This difference in perspective is unavoidable because of the different nature of their activities.

Although this point may seem obvious enough, the issue of multiple perspectives on value creation is actually quite subtle and complex. Here a powerful new construct called the Wholonics model comes in handy, as it gives you a way to categorize value-creation activities within an organization and to understand how leadership style, resource allocation, and performance metrics can all be aligned and customized to serve the needs of the corporate strategy.[2]

The Wholonics Model

The Wholonics model involves four quadrants characterized by action verbs: *control, compete, create,* and *collaborate.* Think of these quadrants as collections of activities that share a particular focus with respect to value creation. Here's a brief introduction to each of the four quadrants.

Control
Value-enhancing activities in this quadrant deal with improvements in efficiency through better processes. The mantra of this quadrant is "Better, cheaper, and surer." A fairly high degree of

statistical predictability is one of the hallmarks of this quadrant. Examples of activities belonging to this quadrant include improvements in manufacturing quality through statistical process control by employing programs like Motorola's Six-Sigma or Whirlpool's Operational Excellence, cost productivity improvements, reduction in manufacturing cycle time, and improvements in product development cycle time. It is the activities in this quadrant that make organizations function smoothly and efficiently.

Compete
Value-enhancing activities in this quadrant deal with being responsive to pressures and signals in the market and with delivering shareholder value consistently. Speed is an essential element of this quadrant. The mantra of this quadrant is "Create shareholder value now and every day." Examples of activities belonging to this quadrant include implementing aggressive measures to reduce working capital (Dell Computers), outsourcing selected aspects of manufacturing to reduce fixed-asset capital investment (Heinz), adopting performance measures like Economic Value (Coca-Cola, Merrill Lynch), divesting business units (Kodak's sales of its health and household products business units), and acquiring other firms (Compaq's 1998 acquisition of Digital Equipment Corporation). The activities in this quadrant help position the firm well with investors by creating a good reputation for delivering consistent financial performance.

Create
Value-enhancing activities in this quadrant deal with innovation in the products and services the organization produces. The mantra of this quadrant is "Create the future." This is the quadrant of discontinuities. Examples of activities in this quadrant include innovative product-line extensions, radical new product

breakthroughs (Sony's development of the Walkman), innovations in distribution and logistics that redefine entire industries (Dell Computers and Wal-Mart), and new technologies (gene splicing and quantum computing). Activities in this quadrant enable the firm to leapfrog its competitors and achieve breakthrough levels of performance. But these activities are also more risky in that success probabilities are typically much lower than those associated with the Control and Compete quadrants. Moreover, the payoff time—how fast results are achieved—in this quadrant is also highly unpredictable.

Collaborate

Value-enhancing activities in this quadrant deal with building organizational competencies by developing people and the right organizational culture. Things get done the slowest in this quadrant. The mantra of this quadrant is "Sustaining the organization through its culture and its people." Examples of activities in this quadrant include implementing organization-wide "culture" initiatives aimed at clarifying organizational values, norms, and expectations; developing employees and cross-functional work groups; and implementing programs to enhance employee retention. Examples are Intel's nonbureaucratic office structure—introduced by former CEO Andrew Grove—in which all employees including the CEO work in easily accessible cubicles, the empowering of field managers by CEO Jack Greenberg at McDonald's Corporation, and the large investments in employee training and development by General Electric and Motorola. It is the activities in this quadrant that help to sustain the organization's ability to create value. But measuring the tangible value created by these activities is also harder than in any other quadrant.

■

Figure 2.3 provides a pictorial representation of the four quadrants. The activities the organization undertakes in each quadrant

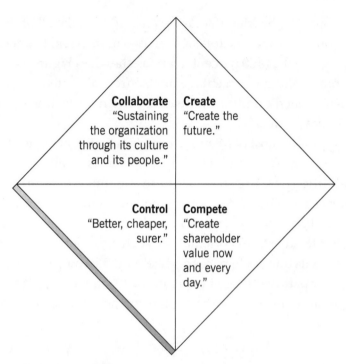

Figure 2.3. The Wholonics Model

create value, but they do so in very different ways. This difference in itself can pose problems, since someone who works primarily in any one quadrant will find it difficult to understand how someone working primarily in another quadrant can add to value. But the problem runs deeper than that—activities that add value in one quadrant are often seen as destroying it in another, and these perceptions may well be correct.

The Relationship of the Four Quadrants to Different Functional Areas

The four quadrants in the model deal with activities within the organization and the resources allocated to them, rather than with functional areas. But since each functional area is a collection of activities, it is not difficult to map functional areas to the four quadrants for illustration purposes.

Consider the Manufacturing area. If you take all of its activities and consider the total resources—human and financial—dedicated to it as 100 percent, then (as shown in Figure 2.4) it is possible to plot the percentage of resources allocated to the activities in each quadrant on each of the four sections of the Wholonics model.

Typically, most of Manufacturing's activities are in the Control quadrant. The focus is on improving costs, quality, and predictability. There are some activities devoted to maintaining employee morale and developing the right culture. These belong in the Collaborate quadrant. Similarly, there are some activities devoted to an external orientation, such as understanding customer needs and preferences and helping the company become more competitive. These belong in the Compete quadrant. But the Collaborate and Compete quadrant activities consume far

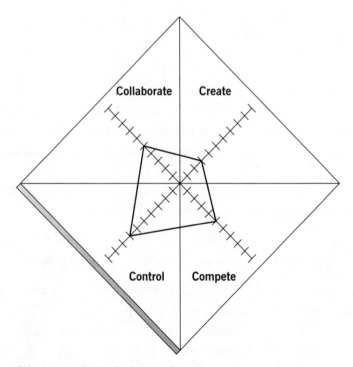

Figure 2.4. A Wholonics Profile for Manufacturing

less organizational resources than those in the Control quadrant. In like vein, there are also resources devoted to manufacturing innovations. To the extent that these are incremental—such as those in most Total Quality Management (TQM) initiatives like the Six-Sigma manufacturing quality improvement programs currently popular at many companies—they belong in the Control quadrant. Breakthrough improvements belong in the Create quadrant. An example is the innovation of Japanese automobile manufacturers that reduced the changeover time involved in shifting manufacturing from one model of car to another from eight hours to less than a minute. However, in most Manufacturing organizations, these activities consume a very small fraction of the total resources.

A profile for Human Resources would look very different, as shown in Figure 2.5.

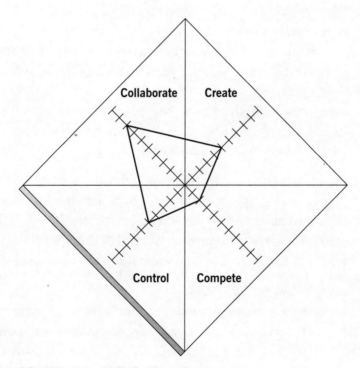

Figure 2.5. A Wholonics Profile for Human Resources

A typical HR group devotes most of its resources to activities in the Collaborate quadrant. These involve building a community within the organization that has the appropriate culture and values. The second-highest allocation of resources typically is to activities in the Compete quadrant. HR operates in the market for human talent, and this requires an external orientation to identify and recruit the best people, as well as to retain them in the face of competing offers from other organizations. Probably the third-highest allocation of resources is to the Control quadrant. HR performs a whole set of transactional activities that fall in this quadrant, such as designing compensation contracts, handling labor union negotiations, and ensuring compliance with fair-hiring and other labor practices. Finally, while HR also gets involved in the creation of breakthrough new products, services, and processes, typically these activities consume the least organizational resources in this area.

Thus every functional area within the organization is likely to have resources allocated to activities in all four quadrants, but the relative allocation of resources varies from one functional area to the next. Moreover, even for a given functional area, the allocation of resources to a particular quadrant varies from one company to the next, depending on the firm's strategy.

Competing Values in the Wholonics Model

An important element of the Wholonics model is that there are *competing values* in any organization. That is, activities in the four quadrants are competing for constrained resources. However, because activities in the four quadrants are very different, it may be hard for many employees to appreciate how they *all* create value.

The Enemy Is Diagonally Across

It is the very nature of the quadrants that value-enhancing activities located in quadrants diagonally across from each other seem to be diametrically opposed. Thus a person who works primarily in the Compete quadrant will typically view many activities in the Collaborate quadrant as destroying value.

The reason for this is simple. People *self-select* themselves in deciding the part of the organization they want to work in and the kinds of activities they want to create value with. Those who work in a functional area focused primarily in the Compete quadrant tend to begin with a predilection for it—and in any case to develop a deeply rooted belief that the best way to add value is by engaging in the activities associated with that quadrant. Further, the *performance metrics* with which they assess the value of any activity are those best suited for the activities in the Compete quadrant. Viewed from the perspective of these metrics, much of what happens in the Collaborate quadrant looks like a waste of resources!

The same logic applies to the Control and Create quadrants. The low success rate and the unpredictability of project completion times that characterize the Create quadrant are abhorred by those whose focus is in the Control quadrant, who pride themselves on a high success rate and predictable project completion times. If those focused in the Control quadrant behaved like those focused in the Create quadrant, they would be considered failures.

Since different functional areas in the organization assign differing degrees of importance to the different quadrants, it is easy to see why they often work at cross-purposes. The vocabulary, mechanisms, and measurement systems of the four quadrants are so different that even if everybody in the organization is creating value, few might believe it.

Any Move in One Direction
Is a Move Away from the Other
One of the classic organizational tensions exposed by the Wholonics model is that any move to allocate constrained resources to one quadrant will be viewed as diminishing the value creation

potential of the quadrant diagonally across, as shown in Figure 2.6. For example, any move toward one quadrant will typically pull the organization away from the diagonally opposite quadrant.

The clan-building activities of the Collaborate quadrant create expenses that detract from value creation as measured by the Compete quadrant, whose metric quite often is short-term, bottom-line financial impact. Similarly, when a corporation responds to the call of the Compete quadrant and restructures itself by laying off a portion of its workforce, those in the Collaborate quadrant see the decision as a reckless destruction of value for short-term gain. In their eyes, it disrupts the organization's culture and can damage employee morale.

The Scott Paper Company is a good example here. The world's largest producer of consumer tissue products had per-

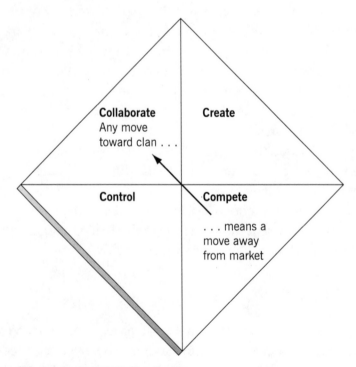

Figure 2.6. One Quadrant Pulls from Another

formed poorly in financial terms for four years in a row, forcing the board of directors to bring in Albert Dunlap as chairman and CEO in 1994. Dunlap responded by substantially restructuring the company, adopting incentive-based compensation, and firing over eleven thousand people. These were classic moves of someone operating in the Compete quadrant, moves that immediately generated substantial shareholder value. But they came across as value destroyers in the Collaborate quadrant because of the number of people fired. It is this perception that the enemy lives in the quadrant diagonally across from you that engenders numerous frictions in organizations.

Although tensions naturally arise in terms of how value-creating activities are viewed in the different quadrants, virtually every organization needs activities in *all four* quadrants. The relative emphases on the different quadrants will depend on the organization's strategy, and will vary from organization to organization. But the lack of activities in any quadrant can prove to be the Achilles heel of any organization. For example, a creative Internet start-up may focus on the Create quadrant at the expense of Control. But as it grows in size and complexity, the lack of common organizational processes can result in inefficiencies, excessive costs, and even destructive chaos. Similarly, a bottom-line–focused company may concentrate on the Control and Compete quadrants at the expense of Collaborate and Create. Although it may deliver results in the short run, it is likely to run out of growth-generating new ideas to build on for the future—and it runs the risk of losing valuable employees because its organization structure is showing signs of corrosion.

Organizational Strategies for Developing
a Multiple Value-Creation Perspective
The Wholonics model provides a simple but powerful tool for diagnosing the way employees perceive value-creating activities

and opening up the possibility of a more nuanced understanding of value. Using the Wholonics model in creative ways in problem-solving exercises with groups of employees can be an effective way to help employees *internalize* the multiple value creation approaches that are essential to an organization's growth and success.

I remember working with a group of about thirty upper-middle-management people from a company that had just gone through a "merger of equals." It was decided that there would be two co-CEOs, one from each of the merging organizations. One CEO's job description was to "attend to emerging new technologies and markets," whereas the other CEO was to manage everything else.

During our discussions, it became clear that everybody in the room thought that the CEO who had been assigned emerging new technologies and markets had been "squeezed out." After all, the other CEO was going to make all the "important" decisions. So wasn't assigning this vague thing called new technologies and markets just a way of providing a graceful exit for the CEO who had apparently lost the battle for control?

At this stage, I decided to engage the group in an exercise designed to help them understand the Wholonics model. The exercise consisted of using a specially constructed deck of cards and having each of the participants pick three cards that best described them and how they contributed value. Based on the chosen cards, each person was placed in a particular corner of the room, with each of the four corners representing a quadrant. When we had four groups formed, each group was given a certain amount of time to read from their cards, with the other groups reacting with comments about how *they* viewed the activities that were being read aloud. Each group was made fun of, but it was all in good humor. At the end of our discussion of each of the groups, the conclusion invariably was that the activities of that group did add value and that they were an essential part of the organization.

Our discussions revealed that while much of the existing value creation in this new company came from products and services that were well understood and developed, competition in those markets was intensifying. Consequently, significant value creation in the future was going to have to come from breakthrough new products—radical departures from the status quo. In fact, in the opinion of some, the merger had been initially conceived as a way to enable such breakthroughs.

Suddenly, there was an almost magical transformation. The group understood that "attending to emerging new technologies and markets" was essential to the growth and perhaps the very survival of the new organization. Moreover, the allocation of tasks between the two CEOs also made sense in light of the four quadrants, since the CEO who was running the organization on a day-to-day basis was essentially attending to activities in the lower two quadrants (Control and Compete), while the CEO who was going to attend to emerging new technologies and markets was mostly going to be leading activities in the upper two quadrants (Collaborate and Create). Most of those in the room felt that this allocation of tasks matched the skills of the two CEOs fairly well.

This experience was by no means unique. In organization after organization, I have discovered that the Wholonics model is a highly effective tool to help people develop a richer and more expansive value-creation perspective. It enables them to categorize their organizations' activities in ways that permit connections to be made across these activities that allow those in all quadrants to appreciate their value-creation potential. For example, I was teaching an executive education program on mergers and acquisitions, and the day before I introduced the Wholonics model the participants had analyzed the Daimler-Chrysler merger and concluded that the disparate cultures made it unlikely the merger would succeed in creating the promised value. After being introduced to the Wholonics model, the participants reached a completely different conclusion. They viewed the merger as bringing together strengths in different quadrants—strengths that would be difficult to integrate, but with the potential to create enormous value.

Beyond its obvious use in helping employees understand the many ways in which value is created, the Wholonics model can also be helpful in making people understand the value of diversity. Strong organizations are formed by individuals with diverse viewpoints. Just as diversity of activities across the four quadrants makes the organization more effective in creating value, so does diversity in people help to create a strong cultural fabric that facilitates sustained value creation.

Personal Strategies for Developing
a Multiple Value-Creation Perspective
There are important value-creation lessons from the Wholonics model at the personal level as well. First, develop an understanding of your strengths and weaknesses in performing activities in the four quadrants. Everyone likes to think that they do everything well. But people who really are competent across the board are rarely found outside of fiction. It is important to know your own self. Which types of activities are you really good at? Which do you really enjoy and spend time on willingly? Which do you like to avoid?

Second, surround yourself with the enemy. Once you discover your strengths and weaknesses, make friends with those whose strengths lie in the quadrants diagonally opposite from those in which your strengths lie. Collaborate with these people. They will help you to be faster and more productive by picking up activities that don't showcase your talents well.

This is hard to do. Most of us tend to gravitate to those who are like us. We have the most in common with them. The problem is that their skills overlap with ours, so that the quadrants we are weak in remain weaknesses.

Third, work on improving yourself in the skills needed to operate effectively in quadrants that are diagonally across from your quadrants of strength.

CHAPTER SUMMARY

Understanding the meaning of value and the different ways in which value can be created are the first two steps in becoming an effective value creator. There are four reasons why understanding of the meaning of value creation often gets blurred: fuzzy definition of value and its drivers, self-interested behavior, negative competition, and functional silos.

There are specific organizational and personal strategies involved in having a clear understanding of the meaning of value creation. Although an organization needs a single clear definition of value, that does not mean there is a unique way to achieve value creation. Indeed, there are numerous ways to create value. The Wholonics model classifies all value-creation activities into four quadrants. The power of this classification is that it exposes where the inherent value-creation tensions lie in an organization, as well as the strength of diversity. With a deep understanding of the Wholonics view of value creation, one can gain valuable multiple value-creation perspectives. Having established this foundation, the next chapter will discuss the remaining three keys to becoming a great value creator.

Reflections and Discussion

Organizational Steps for Achieving a Shared
Understanding of Value and Value-Creating Activities
1. Review the four organizational strategies presented in this chapter for achieving a single clear definition of value and an understanding of value drivers. Assess your organization's performance on each of these four steps and develop an action plan to correct weaknesses.

2. Review the three organizational strategies for discouraging self-interested behavior by employees. Write what your organization should do on each of these steps if you could start from scratch and there were no constraints. Then write down what your organization does at present. Identify the gaps between what should be and what is, and brainstorm steps for closing these gaps.

3. Review the two organizational strategies for avoiding the negative zone of competition. Examine both the explicit and implicit rewards for the employees in your organization. To what extent does this total reward system satisfy the two conditions specified by these strategies? Try to list all the undesirable behaviors the current reward system produces, and indicate how the system could be changed to avoid these consequences.

4. Review the two organizational strategies for avoiding the functional silo mentality. Carefully examine your performance metrics and ask yourself if they truly attend to the entire value chain. Interview or survey employees at various levels to determine whether the organizational reward system encourages value-enhancing outsourcing. Identify opportunities for improvement.

5. Using Figure 2.4 as a model, construct a Wholonics profile that shows how resources are allocated across the four quadrants in your organization as a whole. Is this profile consistent with your strategy? Does each of your functional groups have its own Wholonics profile? If so, how does it compare to the profile that the group should optimally have?

*Personal Steps for Improving Your Understanding
of Value and Value-Creating Activities*

1. Review the personal strategies for (a) being clear about value and (b) overcoming self-interested behavior. Which of these strategies can you implement today? What stands in way of implementing all of these immediately?

2. Assess your own performance on the issue of the negative zone of competition. In the last twelve months, how many solutions have you proposed that were value-maximizing for the organization but diminished resources allocated to your group? How did you publicize them? What

steps can you take in the next twelve months to improve your performance in this area?

3. Review the personal strategies for overcoming a functional silo mentality and for developing a multiple value-creation perspective. Ask six people (two colleagues, two people outside your company whom you interact with professionally, and two close friends or family members) questions about your strengths and weaknesses that will help you construct your own Wholonics profile. In which quadrants are you strongest? In which are you weak? What does your ideal profile look like? How can you use the personal strategies presented in the chapter to move closer to the ideal?

Putting Value Creation into Practice

Strategy, Success Measures, and Speed

U
nlocking the meaning of value and of value-creating activities provides the basic foundation for value creation, but three secrets remain: strategy, measurement, and speed. Unlocking these three secrets will let you apply your new insights in your daily life, both on the job and off.

■ A Deep Understanding of Strategy

As I said in Chapter One, effective value creators have a deep understanding of both their organization's strategy and their own personal strategy for success. For the organization, the overarching goal of value creation can be met only if decision making at all levels is aligned with this fundamental objective. Achieving this alignment of decision making and value creation begins with the formulation and communication of corporate strategy.

It might seem that "everyone knows" the importance of having a clear strategy that is communicated throughout the organization. Yet in a surprising number of cases, the organization's strategy is either poorly formulated or poorly understood by employees. This point was brought home to me forcefully when I was working with a large company on a consulting project. I asked the company's middle managers to work in groups on what I viewed then as a rather straightforward exercise. It involved addressing the following questions:

1. What is your strategy? Describe it in three bullet points or less.
2. What are the key value drivers in your business? How is your strategy linked to these value drivers?
3. How different is your strategy from that of your competitors?
4. How well do you think the people who report to you understand your strategy? Describe how it drives their decisions as well as yours in the direction of creating shareholder value.

I repeated this exercise with many groups, accumulating scores of responses. What I discovered surprised me:

- Most middle managers had a hard time addressing any of these questions in a meaningful way. In particular, they had considerable difficulty in condensing their corporate strategy into a concise, three-bullet-point statement.
- There was significant variance in the strategy statements provided by different groups of managers. In fact, it was

hard to see how all these managers could be describing the same strategy.

- Virtually no group was able to differentiate the organization's strategy from that of its competitors except with superficial and dangerous statements along these lines:

"No company in our industry has our financial resources and therefore no competitor can grow its business the way we are growing ours."

"We have the best products and the best brand equity. No competitor can match that."

"No competitor has our global reach and therefore we are unique in our ability to leverage our global capabilities."

The responses to the exercise showed that the middle-management group in this company had only a fuzzy idea of the corporate strategy. Certainly, these managers did not really understand how the company's strategy was linked to its value drivers in a way that distinguished the company from its competitors and created shareholder value. Middle management—the largest decision-making group in the company—thus made countless decisions that were integrated with the overall strategy more by chance than by design.

When I brought this issue up with senior management, their reaction was a mixture of surprise, bafflement, and anger. They could not understand why their middle managers seemed so unaware of the company's strategy. As the CEO said, "I talk about it in every presentation I make to the company. Copies of my meetings with Wall Street analysts, during which I describe our strategy in great detail, have been distributed to all these managers. Don't they read anything?"

The executives were also a bit annoyed with me. One of them turned to me, handed me a thirty-page document, and said, "I know you've seen this before. But perhaps you should have our managers read this first and then do the strategy exercise."

When I pointed out that the document had been included as part of the reading materials mailed out to the managers before I met with them, the discussion turned to how little their managers seemed to read important company documents!

This experience made such an impression on me that I began to do this exercise with managers from other companies. The results were almost always the same. In fact, a frustrated manager once asked me whether I had taken the company's senior management through the same exercise. Her prediction was that they wouldn't do much better than the middle managers had! Clearly, what I had encountered in the first company was not an isolated problem.

How Strategy Guides Decision Making

Why is the problem of strategy confusion so important? The answer is simple: strategy is all about the allocation of resources. Knowing the company's strategy is what allows managers to make resource allocation decisions that are aligned with the way the company intends to manage its value drivers to create shareholder value. This relationship is shown in Figure 3.1. It is through the choice and management of value drivers that strategy works to differentiate the organization and create Economic Value. A "strategy" that does not function in this way hardly deserves the name.

To understand the relationship depicted in Figure 3.1, consider two competitors, UPS and Federal Express. Both have aggressive global expansion goals, but their strategies for achieving these goals are poles apart. UPS's strategy involves minimizing the use of capital, so it is willing to outsource operational components

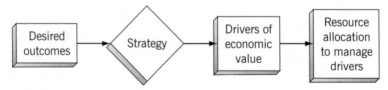

Figure 3.1. From Desired Outcomes to Resource Allocation

that are capital intensive even if doing so entails some loss of control. That's why, when UPS entered China, it decided not to own the fleets of trucks and airplanes it needed to deliver packages. The actual means of delivery was outsourced. Consequently, the key value drivers for UPS were the training of the package delivery partners to whom these tasks were outsourced, the training of UPS employees to work effectively in the Chinese environment, and a corporate understanding of the logistics environment in China. Since these were the value drivers to be managed, adequate resources also needed to be allocated to the activities involved in managing them, such as education aimed at improving the logistics and service capabilities of Chinese employees and partners as well as compensation packages that would create a sense of ownership.

By contrast, Federal Express had a strategy for entering China that was very similar to its domestic strategy in the United States. Its strategy involved owning all the assets, including trucks and airplanes. Consequently, a critical success factor for FedEx is asset productivity, or how efficiently it manages its asset base, as well as whether it has access to an adequate number of air-freight routes between the United States and China. This implies a host of underlying value drivers such as how closely employee compensation is tied to asset productivity, the periods of time over which assets lie unutilized, employee training to optimize both asset utilization and maintenance, negotiating successfully with the relevant governments to acquire the necessary air-freight routes for its planes, and so on. Any manager or executive who understands that these are the underlying value drivers for FedEx will make very different resource allocation decisions from those being made at UPS. For instance, if the problem is to increase customer satisfaction by improving on-time delivery, FedEx may attempt to address it by adding to its fleet of trucks and planes or finding a way to elevate asset productivity. By contrast, UPS is likely to approach it through better training of employees or by acquiring greater capabilities in its delivery partners.

When managers don't have a deep understanding of the organization's strategy, everything else breaks down. It does not matter how experienced they are in the business. It takes strategy to inform a manager about which value drivers to focus on and how to allocate resources to them. Asking managers to carry out their technical responsibilities without imparting a deep understanding of strategy is like asking someone to fly an airplane without specifying a route!

It might seem that a performance metric like Economic Value, which creates incentives for managers to maximize shareholder value, should tackle this problem even if strategy is not well understood throughout the organization. Unfortunately, such reasoning is terribly flawed. A financial performance metric like Economic Value is intended to reward employees for investing in projects that these employees believe will create value for the organization. But regardless of what a project promises on paper, it is unlikely to create the desired value if it is not aligned with the company's strategy. In fact, *it is the purpose of strategy to allow managers to say no to seemingly good projects.* A company doesn't need strategy to turn down projects that managers think are bad. It is strategy that determines the allocation of scarce resources to the highest-value uses.

There are two main reasons why projects that otherwise look good don't deliver the promised value creation when they are misaligned with the company's strategy. One is that the project may be incompatible with the skills and the capabilities of the organization. The other is that its lack of consistency with the strategy could lead the organization to commit fewer resources to the project than the people involved had anticipated.

If two companies have different strategies, then the way they would assess the same initiative may also be different. To see this point, consider the case of Intel, the world's dominant chip maker.

Innovation Without Intuition: Intel

Intel's strategy is to achieve technological breakthroughs in microprocessors and then increase margins by squeezing costs out of the product. The company has a portfolio of products that include low-margin products like the inexpensive Celeron chip as well as higher-margin products like the Pentium line and the Xeon workstation. The company's strategy has been tremendously successful. In 1999, it had over 70 percent of the multibillion-dollar microprocessor market and a 56 percent gross profit margin.

Intel's highly successful strategy has been driven largely by its technical and analytical prowess, skills that inhere primarily in the Control and Compete quadrants. Interestingly, the company itself is organized very much along Collaborate lines, with an open, proactive culture that emphasizes the lack of barriers between various levels of the organization. Founder and ex-CEO Andrew Grove became famous for sitting in a cubicle, just like everybody else, and encouraging employees to stop by to discuss things. This culture notwithstanding, the company's strategic product focus can be described as belonging to the Control and Compete quadrants.

The focus of Intel's strategy was underscored by the way the company responded when its stock price fell by 32 percent between February and June 1998. One of Intel's initiatives was to impose very stringent spending targets. It slashed travel spending by making greater use of videoconferencing. It reduced its headcount by three thousand in 1998 and encouraged customers to place more orders over the Internet to lower processing costs.[1] Another company, focused more on the Create quadrant, might have responded to the drop in stock price by revamping its new product development process.

In a Control-oriented company, initiatives must be judged on the basis of their potential to deliver cost productivity and product feature improvements with a high probability and with reasonably predictable and short cycle times. Decisions should be based on science and sound analytics, not intuition or gut feel. Thus, in coming up with product ideas, highly ad hoc thinking of the sort you might expect in the Walt Disney Company or in a retail-oriented e-commerce company like Greetings.com may not be appropriate. CEO Andrew Grove underscored this point when he said, "Intuition is not going to get you a three-million-transistor microprocessor. We are fundamentally a technology company. We don't make toothpaste."[2]

Strategy, usually driven by the industry context of the company and how it perceives its strengths, can also be *situational.* This means that an organization can find itself in a situation that demands a particular strategy that differs from what it did before, which in turn suggests that a particular quadrant becomes dominant for the new strategy.

Consider the merger of Mellon Bank with Dreyfus Corporation in 1994. Although applauded as the wave of the future for the banking and mutual fund industries, this merger ran into considerable difficulty because the two organizations had radically different cultures. Mellon had a Control-quadrant culture, with a focus on expense productivity.[3] The Dreyfus culture was much more laid back and less performance-driven. The consequences of this culture clash were the loss of key Dreyfus executives, decline in Dreyfus funds' market share, declining fees, deeper cost cutting, and a slowing down of progress on major projects.

A situation like this cries out for a strategic focus that is driven largely by the Collaborate quadrant. What is needed is an identification of the values that people in the new organization want and the culture these values will shape. Such a culture project should be allocated the resources it needs. To evaluate the project, executives would need to tolerate a possibly high level of ambiguity about the time horizon over which benefits would be expected to accrue as well as high uncertainty about the levels of future cash flows attributable to the project. They would not evaluate this project the way one evaluates Dreyfus mutual funds. If they did, the culture project would never get off the ground.

Organizational Realities That Create Disconnects Between Strategy and Decision Making

A primary cause of "disconnects" between strategy and every-day decision making is a traditional view of how corporate strategy should be formulated. There are three aspects of this traditional mind-set that contribute to the problem: secrecy, an ivory-tower approach to strategy making, and complexity.

Secrecy
Traditionally, corporate strategy has been viewed as the near-exclusive domain of senior management. In one company I consulted with, I was working with a group of twenty-five upper-middle managers, representing the top 0.5 percent of the organization. For what we were doing, each person needed to have the company's strategy document. The idea was for us to "take apart" the document and examine its implications for some of the decisions that the group was considering. The company insisted that the document not be mailed to participants in advance of the meeting.

At the meeting, a copy of the document was handed out to each person. The cover page was stamped "Highly Confidential—for limited distribution only." Instructions were given that no copies were to be made during the session. At the end of the session, all the copies of the document were collected and put away. The emphasis was undoubtedly on secrecy.

How can the strategy be understood, internalized, and effec-tively communicated by managers when they are permitted only an occasional glimpse at it? Besides, what sort of a message about trust are you sending if you tell the top 0.5 percent of your people that you can't trust even them with a description of your strategy?

An Ivory Tower Approach to Strategy Making
Many companies have Corporate Strategy groups. Many of these groups are ineffective. Their impact on the organization is limited. The people in the group are rarely promoted to top positions in the organization. Very few people in the organization view them as strategic partners in the business.

When I first observed this phenomenon, I was baffled. The people I met in Corporate Strategy groups were among the smartest in their companies. They had excellent competitive intelligence data. They were skilled at financial analysis. They had read just about every book on strategy.

So why were they ineffective? Because they were basically in an ivory tower, insulated from the rest of the organization. Many of them had never worked outside the Finance and Corporate Strategy groups. They knew almost nothing of organizational politics, the cultural fabric of the organization. The unwritten rules of conduct and the network of informal relationships that exist in every organization have a huge bearing on how resource allocation decisions are made and strategy is executed. To design the company's strategy without having a rich knowledge of these organizational issues is like writing the computer program for traffic lights in an area with no knowledge of the traffic patterns! As a result, in these companies the Corporate Strategy group was (correctly) viewed purely as a "staff support" function. Both its credibility and its effectiveness were limited.

Complexity
For some reason, many companies prefer to describe their strategy with excessively verbose prose. There are very few companies where even senior management does an effective job of addressing the four questions in the strategy exercise I mentioned earlier, particularly when it comes to succinctly describing the strategy in three bullet points.

Complexity is typically the enemy of effectiveness. Few, if any, employees will bother to remember even the gist of what is contained in a thirty-page strategy document, let alone internalize it for day-to-day decision making. Psychologists have noted that a human being's short-term memory can hold at most nine ideas at one time, and typically far less. The fewer ideas you expect employees to hold in their minds, particularly during moments of stressful decision making, the more successful you will be in ensuring that these ideas are remembered.

So why is complexity so ubiquitous? One reason is that simplicity is often much harder to attain than complexity. For example, writers often say that it takes longer to write short. Achieving clarity by paring away unnecessary complications in both thinking and verbiage in order to get to the heart of the matter is hard work. As the English novelist Somerset Maugham once wrote, "To write simply is as difficult as to be good." A second reason is that sometimes people communicate in complex ways to appear profound or to hide their own inadequate knowledge. As George D. Prentice has observed, "Many a writer seems to think he is never profound except when he can't understand his own meaning."[4]

The Traditional View of the Corporate Strategy Group
Too often the Corporate Strategy group in a company has a perception of its role—shared by others in the organization—that is consistent with secrecy, insulation, and complexity. The traditional view of the group is that it is a collection of consultants to the organization who don't need to worry about implementing the strategy. Rather, their job is to help senior management come up with the strategy and provide supporting market and financial analyses. Groups like that often seem less interested in organizational impact than in the intellectual elegance of their analyses.

This narrow perception of the role of Corporate Strategy groups is an important cause of the failure of strategy. Indeed, in many cases neither the group nor the consumers of its work product are even aware of the disconnect between strategy and everyday decisions. In what follows, you will see a more effective role for those involved in corporate strategy.

Organizational Strategy to Link Value Creation, Corporate Strategy, and Decision Making

Maximizing value organizationally means ensuring that day-to-day decision making is linked to strategy, and that the strategy is designed to maximize value creation. The following case study illustrates how this linkage can be accomplished.

Strategic Unity: The Walt Disney Company

In their 1983 book *In Search of Excellence*, Peters and Waterman described the Walt Disney Company as one of the truly excellent companies in the world. The company had a powerful brand identity and seemed uniquely positioned to expand its presence in the entertainment industry.

By mid-1984, however, the company was in turmoil. CEO Ron Miller was under siege, facing a hostile takeover attempt by Saul Steinberg. Although Steinberg was paid greenmail to exit the contest, Miller eventually lost his job as CEO. He was replaced by Michael Eisner.

The Walt Disney Company had many problems under Miller. But perhaps none was more glaring than a misguided strategy of real estate and other acquisitions and insufficient focus on the key value drivers in the business.

Michael Eisner changed all that. He recognized that the key value driver for Disney was its creative output, and the tangible manifestation of that driver was in the making of films. In particular, Eisner saw the enormous potential in animated films. These have long shelf lives and can be very profitably added to Disney's impressive film library.

When Eisner took over as CEO, reporters asked him about his strategy. In the spirit of the "three-bullet-point" format, Eisner described his strategy as making sixteen films during the next year, and that the world should judge him on that basis alone. At that time the company was making four films per year.

Eisner's statement of strategy remains a classic. Why?

- It was simple and concise, so anyone could understand and remember it.
- It was intricately tied to the key value driver for Disney, which was its creative output as manifested in films.
- It specified a quantitative target that the whole organization could be energized behind and that could be used to judge success.
- It clearly specified what the company would do and what it would not do (by stipulating that his singular focus would be on films, Eisner signaled a departure from Miller's real estate acquisition strategy).

This last point is important. Too often you see flowery descriptions of strategy that suggest a wonderful world of possibilities facing the company and all the things it will or might do. But these strategy descriptions are conspicuously silent about what they commit the firm *not* to do. Always be suspicious of strategy statements that do not preclude activities that the company would have engaged in without the strategy statement.

The Disney example shows the importance of a definition of strategy that is linked to key value drivers and that is well understood by most employees. Exhibit 3.1 provides a test of how well your organization's strategy fits the ideal.

The Disney case study and Exhibit 3.1 also suggest a redefined role for those involved in making corporate strategy. Figure 3.2 depicts a process for designing strategy that is geared to ensuring a linkage between strategy, key value drivers, and decision making at all levels of the organization.

In this process strategy makers play a quite different role from the one implied by the traditional view of Corporate Strategy groups. The essential difference is that those involved in strategy make the transition from being in a purely consulting

Exhibit 3.1. Strategy Diagnostic Test

To see whether your strategy is effectively formulated and implemented, subject it to the following questions:

1. How simple is the strategy statement?

2. What are the three most important activities it focuses attention on?

3. Can everyone in the company remember what these three things are without having to refer to a manual?

4. Could you capture the essence of the strategy in a one-minute sound bite for a TV news reporter or an hourly employee?

5. What are the three most important activities that the company would have engaged in without the strategy statement that the strategy now precludes?

6. How much consensus is there in the company that the strategy is right for the company and will create significant shareholder value?

   Below the managerial level: _____

   At the managerial level: _____

   At the level of directors: _____

   At the vice president level: _____

   At the executive committee level: _____

7. How effectively do you believe the strategy has been communicated to various levels in the organization?

8. How effectively has the strategy been linked to performance measures and rewards?

9. Are your business processes and resource allocation consistent with your strategy? If not, where do the gaps exist?

10. How effectively have you put in place mechanisms for supplying strategic feedback at various levels in the organization and for facilitating strategy review and learning?

11. How different is your company's strategy from the strategies of your major competitors?

Source: John Boquist, Todd Milbourn, and Anjan Thakor, *The Value Sphere* (Bloomington, Ind.: VIA Press, 1999).

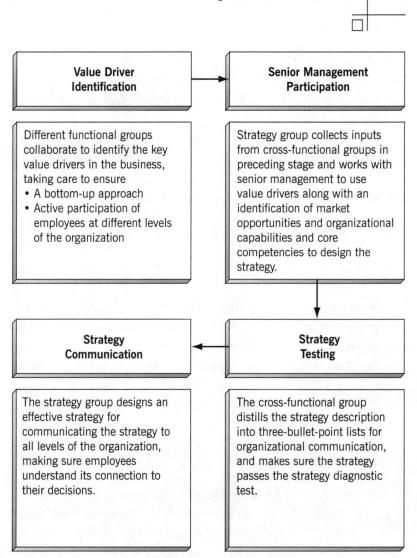

Figure 3.2. Designing Strategy to Maximize Value Creation

role to being responsible for effectively communicating the strategy and facilitating its implementation. This level of involvement and accountability is important for closing the gap between strategy and everyday decisions.

As the figure shows, an essential step in this process is the identification of the key value drivers for a particular organization.

Personal Strategy to Link Your Decision Making to Value Creation

A personal strategy serves the same purpose for you that an organizational strategy does for the organization. It tells you what to focus on and what to avoid. It guides the allocation of your time and effort.

I am reminded of a distinguished colleague who had worked as a professor at the same business school for many years. He had received numerous offers to move to other schools for more money. Many of these offers were from schools that were more prestigious. He'd always turned them down. Some years back, I happened to be appointed to the search committee for a new dean for the business school where I was employed. I called this professor to see whether he had any interest in the job. When he said no, I asked him why. Here is what he said:

> It's not what I want to do. My goal is to focus on my research and teaching, and spend about 20 percent of my professional activity time on consulting with corporations. I have specific objectives in each of these areas. It's deeply satisfying to me to meet the objectives I set for myself in these areas. Being dean would be nice. I could actually be at a school that was run the way I think a school should be run. I would finally have a chance to address some of the nagging frustrations I have had with my school over the years. I think I could make a difference. But all of that would take me away from what truly makes me professionally happy—my research, my teaching, and my consulting. You have to make choices in life. I have made mine.

Like this professor, you need to have a definition of your personal strategy that helps you make choices. It should be consonant with your organization's strategy and yet permit you to distinguish yourself from others in the organization. There are three steps you can take to formulate and implement such a strategy.

First, prepare your own personal statement of strategy. Aim for the simplicity and clarity of Eisner's statement of strategy for Disney.

Second, put your personal strategy statement through a test similar to that in the Strategy Diagnostic Instrument in Exhibit 3.1. Focus on the following key questions:

- How simple is your strategy statement? Can you easily recite it to yourself from memory?
- What are the three most important activities your strategy focuses your attention on?
- What are the three most important activities that you would have engaged in without the strategy statement that you will *not* engage in now?
- What outcomes do you expect your strategy to produce? How are these outcomes linked to your personal definition of value creation? Will you have a sense of great personal achievement if these outcomes are realized?
- What measurement system have you put in place to assess your success in executing the strategy?
- How *different* is your personal strategy from those of your colleagues in the organization?

As you assess your strategy, make sure that you test its "fun quotient." Are the activities you will have to engage in to execute your strategy going to be fun for you? Are they the kinds of activities you do willingly, without a lot of external compulsion?

Also, make sure you have included a "personal growth" component in your strategy. What will you do this coming year to increase your knowledge and skills, apart from what you do on the job? What books will you read? What executive education programs will you attend? Increasing your ability to create value is a vital part of increasing both your sense of fulfillment and your own value to the organization.

Third, identify weekly, monthly, and yearly milestones that, when reached, will signal successful implementation of your strategy. Then determine a "celebration plan" that says how you will reward yourself for reaching each milestone. This continual positive reinforcement is crucial for ensuring that you will persist with the execution of the strategy.

Once your strategy is in place, be prepared to alter it as you receive new information that changes your initial assumptions. Recall that strategy is often situational. Flexibility is an important attribute of successful value creators. Similarly, leave some room on your calendar to experiment with new opportunities as they arrive and to attend to those around you. Effective value creators are opportunists. They are open to trying something new and will jump on opportunities that others may pass up. The more informed you are about your company's strategy and value drivers, the more prepared you will be to recognize these opportunities. Moreover, value creators also create around them an environment that facilitates high performance, and this is achieved by attending to the needs of coworkers.

■ Defining and Measuring Success

Great value creators always have a way to measure their success. They avoid "sunflower management," a term that describes pleasing the boss rather than keeping track of things that bear directly on creating value. When organizations or individuals define success—whether openly or tacitly, by their behavior—in terms of pleasing superiors, then people measure how well they are doing by all the wrong metrics, and they make their decisions accordingly.

Neither a company nor an individual can focus on value creation unless that is how success is defined and measured. By contrast, once people understand what value creation means in their organization and identify the key value drivers, appropriate measures of success are not hard to come by. (This point will emerge more clearly in subsequent chapters, in the context of defining key value drivers in different functional areas.) The key task, then, is to make sure that sunflower management does not get in the way of genuine value creation.

Organizational Tools for Minimizing Sunflower Management

There are various tools that can be deployed at the organizational level to reduce the incidence of sunflower management. Here are four of them:

1. *Reward new ideas and big wins much more than incremental progress.* The personal rewards to individuals for coming up with new ideas that pay off big for the organization should be very high. In fact, the rewards should be *disproportionately* high to provide the appropriate incentives. If an incremental improvement leads to, say, a 2 percent improvement in the company's Economic Value and a new idea leads to a 20 percent improvement, then the personal reward for the employee or team responsible for the new idea should be more than ten times the personal reward for the incremental improvement. And the larger the improvement, the more disproportionately high should be the reward. Thus, if the reward for 20 percent improvement is twelve times the reward for 2 percent improvement, the reward for 40 percent improvement should be more than twenty-four times the reward for 2 percent improvement—not less, despite the temptation to taper off; there's

no such thing as "enough is enough" when it comes to rewarding big wins.

Why? The reason is simple. New ideas that promise potentially large payoffs have relatively low success probabilities compared to initiatives expected to produce incremental gains. The incentive for any individual employee is to avoid devoting time and effort to trying to come up with breakthrough ideas. If these new ideas don't work out—and it's likely they won't—the effort to formulate them looks like a waste of time. Incremental projects are typically more appealing. Moreover, failure on new ideas is often more conspicuous within the organization because these new ideas stand out more from "business as usual." Such failure is usually personally costly for those who promoted these ideas. If nothing else happens, the personal reputations of those involved take a beating. It is to overcome these natural forces working against new ideas with breakthrough potential that you need to provide disproportionately high rewards. Incrementalism is a disease that afflicts many companies, and it takes strong medicine to fight it.

This point is directly related to combating sunflower management. Incremental ideas are usually linear extensions of current practices. Consequently, they generate relatively little opportunity for constructive dissent. Incremental improvements allow managers to keep doing things that are more or less in agreement with the views of their superiors. Sunflower management flourishes without anyone noticing it.

By contrast, breakthrough ideas require new thinking that challenges popular assumptions. Such thinking potentially leads to disagreements and a reexamination of the status quo—and the resulting departures from sunflower management may be perceived as being very costly for individuals. People will almost instinctively try to avoid them. A reward system that encourages big ideas can help counteract such instincts.

2. *Develop an organizational culture that encourages challenge rather than agreement and consensus.* I remember a conversation with a manager who had changed jobs about three months prior to my meeting him. I asked him how he liked his new job and company. Here is what he said:

> It's really quite interesting, and I think I can make a contribution here. But I am beginning to see how different this company's culture is from my last company's. There it was expected that if you made a presentation, someone in the room would get in your face and aggressively challenge your analysis. We all understood it wasn't personal. It was just a way to test the soundness of the assumptions and the thinking behind the analysis. If you passed the test, everybody had confidence that the recommendations made sense. If not, you prevented a mistake from being made.
>
> My first month on the job here, I attended about four such presentations. In each case, I ended up asking the really hard questions because no one else in the room did. I thought nothing of it. But then my boss came to see me at the end of the month and asked me if I was unhappy about something. I was surprised and wondered why he'd think I was unhappy. I hadn't complained to anyone about anything. He said no, it wasn't anything I had said, but just that I seemed somewhat angry during the presentations I'd attended. I was shocked. Not only was my probing at these presentations not appreciated, it was misinterpreted as a sign that I was angry about something! While I was really shocked by this then, now I understand. The organization culture here is much more consensus-driven. People just don't get in your face.

This episode illustrates how stark the differences in cultures can be across different companies. To defeat sunflower management, behavior that challenges individuals as well as organizational practices should not come across as hostile. It should be part of normal conduct. Examples of organizations that are well known for having such a culture are Cisco and General Electric. In fact, John Chambers, CEO of Cisco, is well known for constantly asking those who report to him to give him feedback on the one thing he has done really well of late and the one thing he could improve upon. His behavior sends a powerful signal that the organization encourages dissent and is interested in the truth.

3. *Develop trust.* The single most important ingredient for developing an organizational culture that minimizes sunflower management is *trust*. If employees believe that they will not be hurt by disagreeing with their bosses, they will feel more comfortable expressing their true opinions. Few of us have trouble telling our closest friends and family whatever is on our minds. We trust them and believe the truth is not going to change how they feel about us. Few of us take this sense of security with us to the place where we work.

It is commonly believed that trust can only be built over a long period of time. Certainly, time helps. The longer and better you know someone, the more likely it is that you will trust them. But this belief is also a trap because it immediately suggests that employees cannot trust the organization unless they have been there a long time. What are they supposed to do in the meantime? Be distrustful and keep their views to themselves, perhaps concealing unpleasant but vital truths?

To combat such beliefs, the organization needs to continually emphasize the importance of trust as a part of its culture. A practical way to make this real for employees is to judge employees for promotion to leadership positions based on how well they develop leaders themselves. Developing a leader requires creating an environment in which that person can begin to act like a leader. That means delegating more to that person, leaving room for decisions of real consequence. That takes trust. If employees become convinced that developing leaders in those who report to them is an integral part of how *they* will be assessed, trust grows. Distrust is not an attractive option anymore. Indeed, one of the most effective ways to build trust is to provide strong incentives for managers to delegate to their subordinates decisions they would normally make themselves.

4. *Walk the talk.* Another important weapon against sunflower management is for senior executives to walk the talk. That means that, like John Chambers of Cisco, they should actively seek disconfirming opinions, opinions that go against their own views.

In some organizations, senior managers preach the value of dissenting opinions, but their actions don't support their words. In one company I worked with, there was a great deal of frustration surrounding the profit planning process. This frustration came from the fact that the targets set in the annual profit plan were almost never met. The company consistently underperformed relative to its targets. Senior management was disappointed at this apparent lack of performance because it produced frequent negative surprises and hurt the company's credibility with the financial community, including Wall Street.

When I discussed this problem with middle managers, I was told that it was really senior management that was responsible. One manager put it this way:

> Just look at this year's profit plan. Senior management started the process by telling us we had to come up with a plan to sell 9 million units during the year, a significant increase over last year. We prepared a plan to achieve that level of unit sales. Given our knowledge of the market, we knew that to sell that many units, we'd have to lower our selling price. The plan came back from senior management with the criticism that the profit margin in our plan was not high enough. We explained that achieving a higher margin was simply not realistic if we were going to sell 9 million units without altering either our product line or our brand image. This did little to change senior management's thinking. Their message seemed to be: "You did

not hear us. We want *both* the profit margin and the sales volume we have specified. Work out a plan to get there." It was obvious nobody was interested in hearing about the realities of the marketplace.

Guess what? We gave them a plan they liked. Did it work? Of course not! At the end of the year, we did sell about 9 million units. But the profit margin was just a little below the initial margin we'd built into the plan. It was nowhere close to the higher margin that was in the final plan. So we were right all along, but senior management wouldn't believe us. At the end of the year, the company again underperformed relative to the promise made to Wall Street.

Later, I discussed this issue with one of the senior executives in the company. He admitted that managers had been asked to meet both their profit margin and sales volume targets, but said that this demand was nothing more than setting "stretch" targets and challenging the organization to come up with a plan to meet those targets. Isn't that what good leaders do?

I asked him whether he realized that the managers involved were simply viewing the process of planning as an academic exercise in coming up with the numbers that the senior executives would find acceptable, rather than an opportunity to discover innovative ways to achieve stretch goals. I suggested that they really did not believe the plan would work, and that was probably reason in itself that the plan would not work.

The senior executive was shocked. If that was how the managers felt, why didn't they say so? When I pointed out that perhaps they tried to, but backed off when they felt that they might be viewed as resistant to progress by senior management and that this might damage their careers, he responded, "That's ridiculous. We have never fired anyone in this company for telling the truth."

A couple of months after this conversation, I had an opportunity to meet again with a group of middle managers in this company. I narrated to them what the senior executive had told me and asked them why they were afraid to stand firm. The response was, "He's right. They don't fire you for telling the truth. But it's not getting fired that I'm worried about. It's being made irrelevant."

This episode is an excellent illustration of how sunflower management takes hold and the destructive consequences that result. Senior management preached truth telling and the value of dissent, but its actions spoke louder than its words. Employees believed that if they did not do what senior management wanted, they would be moved to meaningless or less satisfying jobs. Someone else would be found to say yes to senior management.

The issue here is not whether the senior executives in this company really punished those who disagreed with them. What matters is that *employees believed that is what would happen.* As long as that perception existed, it was the reality.

The organizational lesson is that senior executives must go out of their way to impress upon those who report to them that they *value* disagreement. They need to convey that people are responsible for their plan forecasts and that disagreement that eventually leads to a better and more realistic plan will be rewarded. And they must act accordingly.

Personal Tools for Minimizing Sunflower Management

Chapter One touched on ways to overcome sunflower management at a personal level and become a better value creator. Here are five specific tools:

1. *Always tell the truth.* As Winston Churchill said, "The truth is incontrovertible." To avoid being a party to sunflower management, you have to consciously decide you're not going to play the yes-man game. Moreover, you must remember that, as an effective value creator, you're in this for the long run. If you are consistent over time in telling the truth, you will develop

a reputation for integrity. Your opinion will be heard and valued. So don't worry too much if your candor makes you unpopular in the short run.

2. *Use trust as a source of power.* Trust is a powerful weapon against sunflower management. The key is to adopt an attitude of trust yourself and not wait for others to prove that they are deserving of your trust.

Human beings have a remarkable capacity to sense trust in those they are interacting with. People sometimes try to disguise the fact that they don't trust the person they are dealing with, but simulating trust usually doesn't work. However, if you genuinely trust people and assume that they have every reason to trust you, the trust between you and those around you is likely to go up significantly. A person who is trusting is easier to trust.

This means that you can use trust as a source of power— not the kind of "power" that comes from manipulating others but the kind that comes from being genuinely trusted. But cultivating trust will not always be easy. *Distrusting* others is a survival instinct honed by millions of years of evolution. You need to learn to consciously override it. And you may not be as patient with those who are slow to discard their own distrust.

3. *Be sure of yourself.* Another way to combat sunflower management is to develop personal confidence. The more sure you are of yourself, the easier it will be for those around you to express their disagreement with you, and the easier it will be for you to be persuasive when you disagree with others.

I remember an interesting conversation with a bank president. The bank was part of a holding company that had just hired a new CEO. At a meeting of the holding company's executive committee, the new CEO asked everyone what they thought the organization's new strategy should be. Nobody spoke up. Obviously, they thought, the new CEO had come in with his own strategy. He was asking them for their opinions just so that he could tell whose views were similar to his own and to identify like-minded executives.

But this CEO turned out to be different. He really did want to know what the other executives thought. When the bank president who told me this story first realized this, he said, his immediate reaction was, "Oh my God! He really *doesn't* know what our strategy should be. Is he not as competent as we thought?"

Eventually the executives came to appreciate the utter honesty of their new CEO. They also came to understand that he sought the opinions of others not because he didn't know what to do but because he had such enormous confidence in his own ability that he did not feel threatened by views that differed from his own. So he was always willing to seek diverse opinions in order to improve his decisions.

Such self-confidence does wonders in inspiring those around you to express their views honestly. It also makes it easier for you to express honest disagreement with others, since they know it is OK to disagree with you.

4. *Don't just disagree, suggest a better way.* I was once a consultant to a team that a company had assembled to work on a major initiative. We met about once a month for two days at a time. The project lasted approximately three months.

One of the team members particularly interested me. She was always the last person to speak on any issue, but her views were almost always different from those of the rest of the team. In other words, she seemed to disagree a lot with the other team members.

Frequently people who habitually voice dissenting views come across as obnoxious. They generate dislike, which in turn diminishes their effectiveness. But not so with this manager. She was very likeable and her team members always respected her views. Why was such a seemingly contrarian person so effective?

The secret to her effectiveness was threefold. First, she was always very pleasant and never made her disagreement come across as a personal criticism of those who spoke before her. She invariably started with something like, "You know, I think these are all really terrific ideas, but I was wondering if I could add one more to the list. . . ." Second, she never seemed offended if the group did not accept her views. Since she herself did not take personal offense when others disagreed with her, it was hard for them to be offended when she disagreed with them. Third, and most important, she never *just* disagreed. She always had a better idea to suggest. This helped focus the group's attention on the pros and cons of the various ideas, rather than on the fact that she had disagreed with the other people on the team.

Disagreeing with others takes tact, but tact alone is not enough. If you only dissent from others' ideas and offer nothing better in their place, then your criticism is likely to seem merely destructive and may well be taken personally. Sometimes it may be best to hold your fire until you can propose a solution you think is better. When you couple your dissent with an alternative idea, you are far more likely to come across as constructive in your criticism and to focus attention on the real issues.

5. *Don't just meet organizational expectations, produce delight.* Every great value creator I have encountered had a personal definition of success that went well beyond what the organization expected of them. Great value creators are internally driven to meet targets they set for themselves. They don't settle for what someone else defines as a target for them.

Such internal motivation is incredibly empowering. If you have it, you will feel you are in control. If you don't, you're likely to feel that others—your boss or your environment—control you. With this internal motivation, you will be driven by your own ambition and goals. You may volunteer for tasks that others consider too challenging or not rewarding enough. Distinguishing yourself from others becomes much easier.

The beauty of setting your own performance targets in this context is that it automatically combats sunflower management. Since you are not driven by the sycophantic desire to please your boss, making that one of your goals is not even an option.

The other consequence of being driven from within is that you will usually exceed the targets others set for you. It will no longer be a struggle for you to keep up with what the organization demands of you. You are always aiming for something bigger, better, and more inspiring. You will be like a marathon runner in a race others expect will cover only a mile. When you achieve *their* target, you will not even be breathing hard!

■ Developing Speed

Developing speed at either the organizational or personal level requires the use of specific tools. This section discusses these tools and how they differ depending on whether it is the organization or the individual that employs them.

Organizational Strategies for Developing Speed

As discussed in Chapter One, there are two keys to improving the speed of an organization. One is by redesigning the resource allocation process and other organizational processes to improve speed. The other is by changing the organization culture so that it becomes more tolerant of failure. Here is a brief discussion of some ways in which this can be done.

Process Redesign
Designing decision-making processes that emphasize speed involves the following key steps:

- *Make sure that people understand the corporate strategy well so that the process is not bogged down by ideas that are not aligned with the strategy.* Oftentimes, ideas that look good on paper turn out to be inconsistent with the corporate strategy. These ideas are dropped after a thorough analysis of the proposals. But they have done their damage in terms of tying up the time and attention of executives who could have more fruitfully devoted these resources elsewhere. The more such bad ideas receive serious consideration, the slower the organization becomes because these ideas are distractions from value creation. The antidote is to have a deep and shared understanding of strategy that minimizes the number of such ideas bubbling up for review.

- *Reward in a big way ideas that are truly innovative compared to what the competition is doing.* This encourages speed because the longer a good idea stays in the process pipeline the less likely it is to look innovative when it is finally approved. In other words, the personal rewards to employees for a big win should be more than proportionate to the magnitude of the win.

- *Be prepared to break up the organization on a regular basis.* Every large organization is prone to being slowed down by bureaucratic processes because Control quadrant activities grow more and more important in any large organization. To minimize the potential damage from this, large organizations should constantly strive to break up into smaller pieces by spinning off divisions as separate entities. This will allow individuals in the spun-off divisions to have more powerful ownership incentives because their compensation can be directly tied to the stock prices of their divisions, and divisional stock prices will be much more sensitive to the efforts of individual employees than the stock price of the conglomerate parent could ever be. And this means greater personal gains to these employees from being faster in their decisions.

- *Create organizational processes that emphasize speed over accuracy.* For example, in resource allocation, many companies have tollgate processes whereby any capital request has to be approved at various stages in the development of the project. The idea is that more information is collected as the project moves through the different stages of development before a final decision is made on whether to approve the capital request to manufacture and market the product.[5] Thus, at each tollgate, someone decides whether to kill the project or continue to the next stage. If it continues, people collect yet more information and move to the next tollgate, where there's another decision to stop or to continue. The amount of time it takes for the project to move from one tollgate to the next depends on how much additional information is required at the next tollgate. One way to speed up the process is to demand less information and be tolerant of greater imprecision.

Organization Culture
Speed requires a greater tolerance for mistakes. Designing a more risk-tolerant organization culture is something a lot of companies talk about, but few are able to do it effectively. The difficulty is that it is not easy to distinguish between errors made by individuals because of a lack of ability and those made in the interest of speedier decision making. Thus it is hard to avoid revising your assessment of a person's ability downward when you observe a failure. Along with this downward revision are diminished monetary rewards and lower chances of promotion for the individual. Knowing this, employees recognize that all the corporate preaching about the value of taking risks is just that—a lot of talk, rhetoric that is not rooted in the organization's punishment and reward systems.

One way to overcome this is to adopt the approach Jack Welch has used at General Electric. To groom future leaders, he gives them divisions or business units to manage with a significant amount of autonomy. The message is, "Go and run this billion-dollar business and see what you can do. Don't be paralyzed by the possibility of failure."

When an organization adopts an approach like Jack Welch's, it is important to remember that those who fail in such ventures should not be punished, either explicitly or implicitly. And remember that punishment doesn't have to involve firing the individual—being made irrelevant (that is, losing the trust of seniors and being put into a job that lacks real authority) is often seen as just as significant a punishment as getting fired, or more so.

Another approach is to have the senior leaders of the organization be continuously involved in teaching others in the organization about the real costs and benefits of risk taking and speed in the organization. Real examples of individual successes and failures within the organization should be candidly discussed.

Personal Strategies for Developing Speed

In studying effective value creators, I have discovered that there is a recipe that enables them to produce high-quality output faster than others. The recipe has two ingredients: parallel processing and the ability to focus and finish.

Mastering the Art of Parallel Processing
Most people process tasks sequentially. They start on a task, finish it, and then move on to the next one. By contrast, the best value creators are good at parallel processing. That is, they can simultaneously work on many different projects. Typically, these projects are at different stages of development. The idea is that every project has its "natural breaks," for example, when you must wait for some information to arrive or for someone to do something that is necessary to move the project forward. Value creators use this time to work on one of the other projects in their portfolio. Or sometimes they switch from one project to another simply to refresh themselves and recharge their batteries. In this way there is no slack time, no time wasted sitting around waiting for something to happen.

Figure 3.3 shows how sequential and parallel processing typically work. For simplicity, it shows a two-task example—but the best value creators parallel process many tasks at once.

Any complex task can be divided into logical phases. Often there is "dead time" between two phases because you are waiting for something else to happen because you are mentally fatigued and need a break. With sequential processing, during this time you usually take a brief respite and typically make no progress. By contrast, with parallel processing, you move back and forth between tasks. This not only eliminates dead time, but

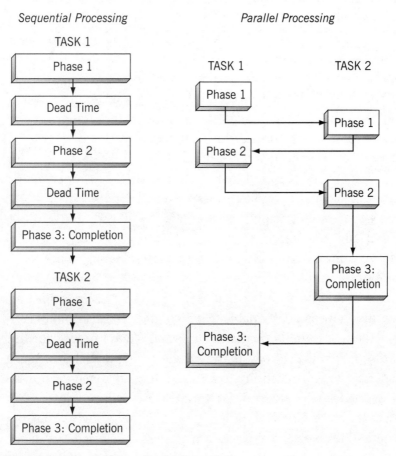

Figure 3.3. Sequential Versus Parallel Processing

also keeps you from being worn out by the monotony of working on the same task for too long. Sometimes a change of activity is actually a better antidote for fatigue than merely resting or chatting with a coworker.

Ability to Focus and Finish
Even with many irons in the fire, great value creators focus like a laser beam on the task at hand. They exhibit an ability to devote all their concentration and energy on the project they are working on at any given moment without being distracted by all the other projects in their portfolio. When they switch their attention to the next project, they once again make it their sole focus and put the first project out of their minds.

For most people, this is the hardest part of parallel processing. Having initiated multiple projects, they lack the ability to concentrate on any one of them because of the distractions created by their other projects. That is why when most people think of speed, they think of progressing faster through a vertical sequence of tasks (and it is also one reason why gaining speed can seem to imply sacrificing quality). When great value creators think of speed, they take the vertical sequence and arrange it *horizontally*, so they can parallel process.

I remember a conversation with a CEO of a Fortune 500 company who had risen to that position in his early forties. I asked him what accounted for his success. He said that the answer was simple. When he and his boss set his annual performance targets, he always asked for a target that he knew his boss would view as unattainable. He then made a career out of *beating* those seemingly unattainable goals. When I probed further, I discovered that he had mastered the art of parallel processing and cultivated the ability to focus with great concentration on the precise task at hand. He said this made him an excellent "closer," someone who finished tasks rather than just starting them. Effective value creators are masters at "closing out" tasks.

The ability to focus reminds me of a wonderful old story. A king had five sons who were being trained in archery by a master archer. After having trained the five princes for some time, the master archer brought them to an open field for their final test. He asked the oldest prince to step forward and shoot an apple on a nearby tree with his bow and arrow. When the prince was on the verge of shooting, the master asked him what he saw. The prince described the blue sky, the mountain behind the apple tree, the branches of the apple tree, and then the apple he was about to shoot. The master waved him aside, telling him it was unnecessary to shoot the arrow. The prince had already flunked the test.

One by one, each of the princes went through the same experience. Each described what he saw the moment before unleashing an arrow at the apple. What each saw was different, but all of them observed a variety of things in and around the apple tree. And each was flunked without being given the opportunity to shoot the apple.

Finally, it was the youngest prince's turn. When the master asked him what he saw, he said, "I see the apple."

"And what else do you see?" asked the master. "Nothing else. I see only the apple," replied the prince. "Then go ahead and shoot," said the master. The prince proceeded to pierce the heart of the apple with his arrow.

The moral of this story is simple. All but the last prince lacked true focus when they were about to shoot the arrow. The master archer knew that this lack of focus doomed them to failure. The only prince who was allowed to shoot was the one who saw the target—and nothing else.

CHAPTER SUMMARY

This chapter covered the three remaining secrets of successful value creators: gaining a deep understanding of strategy, developing measures of success, and mastering speed. If you have a deep understanding of your organization's strategy, you will be able to summarize in three bullet points or less what your strategy is, what key value driver in the business it is tied to, and how it distinguishes your organization from competitors. Moreover, you will have a personal strategy that focuses your attention on what is most likely to make you successful, as well as personal measures of success that assess genuine value creation and keep you from falling prey to sunflower management. To master speed, an organization must develop the appropriate processes and organization culture, whereas an individual must learn the arts of parallel processing and focus.

Although this chapter describes each of these secrets as independent, there are interrelationships among them as well. Having a deep understanding of strategy makes it easier to gain speed in decision making. Developing meaningful measures of success improves your ability to effectively execute your strategy.

In the following chapters, you will see how to use the three secrets unlocked in this chapter and the two secrets discussed in the preceding chapter in the context of specific functional areas within an organization. You may wish to skip to the one describing your own area, but it would be useful to read them all. I believe each chapter is relevant to you regardless of your functional area, because of the enormous benefit to be derived from developing multiple value-creation perspectives.

Reflections and Discussion

Organizational Steps for Effective Strategy, Success Measures, and Speed

1. Take three groups of five to six people, with each group representing a different level in your organization, ideally senior management, upper-middle management, and middle management. Have each group identify what it believes are the key value drivers for your organization. Afterward, compare the value drivers identified by each group. What did you learn? How much consensus is there about the value drivers? Are the identified value drivers consistent with the strategy? What do you need to do?

2. Now ask each group to fill out the Strategy Diagnostic Test in Exhibit 3.1. Again compare the results of the exercise across the three groups, extract the important insights, and determine what needs to be done. In particular, is there a *shared understanding* of the strategy? Have people at different levels internalized it in their decision making?

3. Have senior management in your organization use the results of the exercise in item 2 to arrive at a three-bullet-point description of your strategy that is widely communicated throughout the organization. Develop training programs to help different groups in the company understand what the strategy means for their day-to-day decisions.

4. Critically examine the most visible senior executive promotions in your organization in the last five years and answer the following questions: How many new ideas and big wins were these individuals who were promoted personally responsible for? Were these individuals well known in the organization for constructive disagreement or for consensus? How effective were these individuals in developing trust within their parts of the organization? Use the answers you come up with to assess how prevalent sunflower management is within your organization.

5. How many days does it take for your organization to make a major decision? Interview at least ten employees at various levels in the organization and from different functional areas to discover the *process* and *attitude* impediments to improving organizational speed. Develop an action plan to eliminate these impediments.

Personal Steps for Effective Strategy, Success Measures, and Speed

1. Use the steps outlined in this chapter for creating a personal strategy to formulate your own strategy statement. If you have not already done so, take the time to list ten activities for overcoming self-interested behavior, as described in Chapter Two. Make sure that these activities are part of your strategy.

2. Review the five personal tools for minimizing sunflower management presented in this chapter. Reflect on the past year and identify at least one instance corresponding to each of these tools where it would have been extremely difficult to take the recommended step. What personal changes will you need to make to use these tools consistently?

3. Over the next month, apply the approach to parallel processing described in the chapter to at least two major tasks. Gradually expand the number of tasks you are parallel processing to achieve maximum speed in your job without sacrificing quality. Remember to combine strategies for maximizing speed with strategies for "outsourcing" work that can be done at least as well by others.

Improving
Value Creation
in Procurement
and Manufacturing

T he power of manufacturing excellence in providing a company with a significant competitive edge has long been unquestioned. For firms in many manufacturing industries, such as home appliances and automobile components, materials, and manufacturing costs account for over 75 percent of total cost. Thus misalignment between the way decisions are made by the Procurement and Manufacturing functions and the way decisions should be made to optimize value creation can be very damaging. This chapter applies the five keys to value creation in the specific context of the Procurement and Manufacturing functions.

□

■ What Does Value Mean to You and Your Organization?

Self-interest can obscure the meaning of value even in Procurement and Manufacturing. This happens despite the precise performance metrics that are available to judge both individual and organizational performance.

My favorite example of how self-interest in Procurement and Manufacturing can diverge from what is best for the organization concerns a vice president of an American company who was in charge of a region of Europe and who was based in Germany. The company had manufacturing operations there, and it was becoming noncompetitive in its cost structure. I asked the vice president why he did not recommend that the company move its manufacturing operations from Germany to somewhere in southern Europe, where labor costs were quite a bit lower. He hemmed and hawed on this issue for a while before I discovered the real reason why he found this suggestion unpalatable. Southern Europe was outside his jurisdiction. If manufacturing facilities were moved there, he would have fewer people directly reporting to him. This reduction in his direct reports would lead to a decrease in the midpoint of his salary range. It would also diminish his status within the company. There was no way he was going to make this recommendation even though it would have created value for his organization.

To discover the pervasiveness of the problems created in Procurement and Manufacturing by blurred definitions of value, I began to conduct surveys of managers from different companies. The industries to which these companies belong include manufacturing, financial services, information services, and information technology. The resulting data suggest that these problems are quite widespread.

Research Findings for Procurement

As described in Chapter Two, there are four main reasons that the understanding of value becomes blurred: the fuzzy definition of value and its drivers, self-interested behavior, negative competition, and functional silos. Table 4.1 summarizes the way the majority of my survey respondents in Procurement viewed value creation—and shows many of these problems at work.

The table does indicate a clear definition of value, one that is focused on cost and quality, and a reasonably clear set of the value drivers. However, it also appears that those surveyed did not feel that the value drivers were appropriately identified by their organizations. They viewed cost control pressures as leading to material cost "take out" initiatives that damaged their relationships with suppliers. This is another variant of the negative zone of competition. Instead of promoting the development of deep collaborative relationships with suppliers, the metrics by which Procurement managers are judged are inducing them to engage in zero-sum competitive games with suppliers, which does not foster value-enhancing relationships. Moreover, these managers would like the performance metrics for Procurement to generate stronger incentives to participate in new product development activities.

Value is also destroyed through self-interested behavior that takes the form of making payments to suppliers before the budget period ends, so that the budget can be more fully spent. Similarly, the functional silo mentality is manifested in not working closely with Finance for hedging materials prices.

Research Findings for Manufacturing

Table 4.2 summarizes how the majority of those in Manufacturing viewed their role in value creation.

As in the case of Procurement, it appears that those in Manufacturing have a good idea of the key value drivers they should control, although there is some confusion about value drivers and outcomes. For example, an *outcome* like lower manufacturing costs is viewed as a *value driver*. It is also interesting that the performance metrics that are typically used for Manufacturing

Table 4.1. Procurement's Role in Value Creation

What performance metrics do you typically use?	How does your Procurement group create value? What are the value drivers you control?	How do you destroy value?	How do the financial goals of the company impede value creation by Procurement?	How would you like to redefine these financial goals?
▪ Material cost productivity ▪ Quality improvement	▪ Lowering material costs through aggressive negotiations with suppliers ▪ Consistently delivering quality improvements by using statistical process control techniques ▪ Delivering new features in components demanded by innovations in the design of the company's products ▪ Relationships with vendors	▪ Excessively aggressive negotiations with vendors and suppliers that conflict with supplier innovation incentives ▪ Early payments to suppliers before budget period ends ▪ Not working closely with Finance to develop appropriate strategies for hedging materials prices	▪ Short-term focus on financial projects drives material cost "take out" initiatives with negative consequences for supplier relationships	▪ Shift emphasis to role played by Procurement in new product introductions

Table 4.2. Manufacturing's Role in Value Creation

What performance metrics do you typically use?	How does your Manufacturing group create value? What are the value drivers you control?	How do you destroy value?	How do the financial goals of the company impede value creation by Manufacturing?	How would you like to redefine these goals?
■ Manufacturing defects ■ Warranty costs ■ Total cost productivity ■ On-time delivery	■ Improving product quality through initiatives such as Statistical Process Control ■ Lowering manufacturing cycle time through improved factory layout ■ Headcount reduction ■ Capacity increases ■ On-time new product launches ■ Improving fixed asset utilization ■ Lowering inventory levels ■ Lowering manufacturing cost	■ Products of inadequate quality ■ Failure to launch new products on time ■ Poor cost control ■ Failure to optimally outsource manufacturing or locate manufacturing in the appropriate locations ■ Large capital investments ■ Manufacturing products customers don't need, including over-engineered products ■ Excessively bureaucratic processes	■ Delayed approvals of investment proposals ■ Cost cutting makes quality a constant issue ■ Inadequate staffing	■ Reduce focus on payback and take a more long-term perspective

are viewed as inducing a short-term orientation, as in the case of Procurement. This suggests that assessing Procurement and Manufacturing *solely* by means of Control quadrant performance metrics does *not* maximize value creation, in the opinion of the respondents. Besides, standard performance metrics like manufacturing defects and warranty costs do not provide the appropriate incentives for employees to optimize the use of capital. As a result, a key element of the Compete quadrant is missing in the standard metrics used for Manufacturing, and this may be distorting behavior away from value maximization.

It also seems clear that those in Manufacturing see the financial pressures imposed on them by the company as standing in the way of value creation. Sometimes this is viewed as taking the form of being denied capital. At other times, it is viewed as taking the form of being denied manpower resources due to headcount reduction requirements. In either case, there seems to be lacking a common understanding of the optimal use of the tools of value creation for Manufacturing.

The survey results also provide examples of self-interested behavior and the negative zone of competition such as the failure (unwillingness?) to optimally outsource manufacturing operations or to locate them in the appropriate places. The functional silo mentality is reflected in overengineered products that customers don't need. Interestingly, bureaucratic process, an essential part of the Control quadrant, is viewed as a value destroyer when taken too far.

Thus, it appears that the four reasons that obscure the understanding of value creation in the general case also play important roles for those in Manufacturing.

■ Multiple Value-Creation Perspectives

Traditionally, Procurement and Manufacturing are functions that have been positioned largely in the Control quadrant of the

Wholonics model. This makes the development of multiple value creation perspectives quite challenging for these functions. During much of the post–World War II era, the Procurement and Manufacturing functions in most organizations were driven by two simple goals—improve quality and lower cost. During the 1970s and 1980s, Japanese manufacturers (particularly in the automobile industry) added another goal—reducing *manufacturing cycle time,* or increasing speed. Value drivers were identified to achieve these outcomes and managing these drivers enabled companies to optimize on the basis of process improvements and scale economies.

The Japanese model was successfully imitated in the 1980s and the 1990s by Korean companies. For many of these companies, the common determinant of success was manufacturing prowess. Unfortunately, this led to the emergence of three problems that often keep Procurement and Manufacturing from developing a sufficiently deep appreciation of multiple value-creation perspectives: a "manufacturing is king" mind-set, a tendency for manufacturing prowess to lead to poor product decisions, and a lack of effective communication between Procurement and Manufacturing on one hand and the rest of the organization on the other.

The "Manufacturing Is King" Mind-Set

The global computer memory-chip business, a market pioneered by Intel, provides an excellent example of the "manufacturing is king" mind-set. Faced with intense competition from low-cost Japanese manufacturers, CEO Andrew Grove decided to withdraw from this market. This move was part of a general phenomenon as Japanese giants like Toshiba and NEC Corporation brought the U.S. semiconductor industry to its knees in the 1980s.

In the 1990s, however, Korean companies like Hyundai Electronics Industries used the Japanese model of aggressive pricing and constant investment in new factories to wrest considerable market share away from the Japanese. The significance of this shift in market-share dominance was underscored by the size of the global memory-chip market. It was $22 billion in 1995 and is expected to reach $170 billion by 2005. By that time, memory chips are expected to account for nearly a third of all sales to the semiconductor industry. No wonder NEC vice president Shigeki Matsue lamented, "Now I understand the feelings of U.S. semiconductor companies in 1984."[1]

One reason for Korea's success was technical excellence. Korean companies recruited heavily among South Korean graduates from U.S. universities and South Koreans working for Silicon Valley chipmakers. These engineers were not only technically well trained but were also creative.

A second reason was the willingness of Korean companies to invest huge amounts of capital in new factories. These factories typically require investments exceeding $1 billion each, and they become obsolete in three years or less. Exemplifying this business model is this statement by Yoo Kook Sang, corporate planning director for Hyundai Electronics Industries, "The Japanese hesitated, and now they are falling behind Korean companies. We shall invest continuously without hesitation."[2] This sentiment was echoed by Chin Dae Je, head of memory products at Samsung: "If we stop investing, we cannot grow. Then we'd fall behind in the technology, and perhaps we couldn't recover at all."[3]

This money-losing but market-share-grabbing approach served the Koreans well in terms of elevating their presence in the memory-chip market. But this strategy was largely a pursuit of scale economies and market share without regard for shareholder value. It resulted in massive overinvestment and eventually contributed to the stagnation of the Japanese and South Korean economies in the latter half of the 1990s.

Prior to this stagnation, manufacturing success stories like the Korean chip-making operations were highly celebrated. Consequently, Manufacturing was king, supported by Procurement.

A lot of performance metrics were developed based on this model, including the ones shown in Tables 4.1 and 4.2.

Manufacturing Success Leads to Poor Product Decisions

This historical dominance of Manufacturing and the performance metrics used in assessing it sometimes leads to poor decisions about products. This happens in the following ways:

- *Process improvements and cost efficiency become more important than product innovations.* After all, it's easiest to make manufacturing process improvements when you understand the process and the product well. This is usually true for well-established products and rarely true for new products, leading to a Manufacturing preference for existing products.
- *The not-invented-here syndrome takes over.* It begins to seem that anything that is not manufactured by the company is unacceptable. This leads to a reluctance to outsource even when doing so could create more value than manufacturing within. And it also leads the company to overinvest in manufacturing assets.
- *Overengineering replaces filling customer needs.* Many highly engineered products enjoy high profit margins. The allure of such margins often creates a fondness for adding features in products, which has caused many companies to create products with more features or functionality than customers demand.

This mind-set has further reinforced the Control quadrant positioning of Procurement and Manufacturing. However, in the last two decades, the focus of many firms has shifted from manufacturing excellence to customer satisfaction, particularly in industries that deal with retail customers. There has also been greater pressure to think about shareholder value rather than just manufacturing excellence. The result has been a need to bring more of a Compete quadrant approach to manufacturing. In many companies, including Cisco, Nike, Sara Lee, and Heinz, this shift has led to an outsourcing of much of manufacturing. In other companies, including Herman Miller Furniture and SPX, it has led to the adoption of more comprehensive measures of value creation that resemble Economic Value. In many companies where this has not been done, problems such as those described in this chapter still remain.

Lack of Effective Communication

A classic tension that exists in some organizations is that the Marketing group is often the source of many useful new product ideas, but these ideas must be executed by Manufacturing. The problem is that many of those in Marketing operate primarily in the Create quadrant, whereas those in Manufacturing are mostly in the Control quadrant. Since these two groups have such different views of value creation, they often do not communicate very effectively.

One consequence is that the products that Manufacturing churns out may not match up well with what customers would like. Perhaps the best example is the challenge that recently retired CEO George Fisher faced at Kodak. The company was traditionally dominated by an engineering mentality—that is, products must be developed first, and then buyers can be found. It's the old adage, "Build a better mousetrap and the world will beat a path to your door." In today's customer-focused economy, this approach can lead a company to develop products that are not terribly competitive. While this problem is often easy to recognize, it tends to be much harder to change the organization to become more customer-focused and market-driven. Even after Fisher's retirement, Kodak is still struggling with this transition.

The challenge for Procurement and Manufacturing, then, is to overcome their strong Control quadrant orientation and let their decisions be guided by a greater appreciation of other value-creation perspectives that exist within the organization. As the survey results in Table 4.2 indicate, many of those in Manufacturing view the excessive Control quadrant focus of their organizations as destroying value. The implication is that Procurement and Manufacturing should seek to make a transition from their current Wholonics profile in the direction depicted in Figure 4.1.

What this diagram shows is that Procurement and Manufacturing need to divert greater resources to being more externally focused on customer and shareholder value so as to improve their

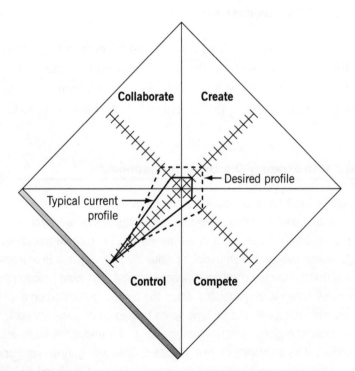

Figure 4.1. The Desired Evolution of Procurement and Manufacturing in the Wholonics Perspective

strength in the Compete quadrant and also be more directly involved in new product development, which is a more long-term Create quadrant activity. Additionally, greater attention also needs to be focused on Collaborate quadrant activities designed to build value-focused, high-performance teams.

These observations are consistent with the survey results in Tables 4.1 and 4.2. Those in Procurement felt that they could create greater value by being more directly involved in new product introductions. Those in Manufacturing wanted their organizations to take a more long-term perspective on value creation, shifting the focus away from headcount reductions and excessively bureaucratic processes that diminish the contribution of the Collaborate quadrant to value creation.

■ What Is Your Business Strategy?

In many companies, the Procurement and Manufacturing strategy becomes disconnected from the overall corporate strategy. An example is what happened to the McDonald's Corporation in the years leading up to the appointment of Jack M. Greenberg as CEO.

Coping with Strategy Disconnects: McDonald's

McDonald's has been enormously successful as a global fast-food franchiser based on its model of serving standardized products that are always above a minimum-quality threshold and are served fast in clean surroundings. It has generated substantial shareholder value through a global Procurement function that selectively combines global sourcing with local procurement. Enormous savings were generated when the company decided on a global procurement strategy for the sesame seeds that go on its buns. By contrast, beef is sourced regionally rather than globally, to improve the freshness of the product. The insistence on beef quality is unwavering, however. For example, when McDonald's opened its first restaurant in Thailand in 1985, it had not yet developed local sources for beef that met its quality threshold. Beef was, therefore, sourced from Australia.

However, intense competition, a stagnant menu, and consumer perceptions that rivals like Burger King were providing higher-quality products led to below-average stock price performance in the mid-to-late 1990s. A very important component of the company's value chain—the manufactured product itself and how it was served in restaurants—was proving to be the company's Achilles heel.

In 1998, the company's menu was ranked by consumers as among the worst-tasting of any restaurant chain. The company had not introduced a successful new product since Chicken McNuggets in 1983. Food was stored in warming bins that adversely affected its flavor. Further, any "custom order" that deviated from a standard product was poorly processed. There was thus a disconnect between the strategy of being a brand-driven, customer-focused company that attended to the needs of the marketplace and what the company was producing.

Around this time, Jack M. Greenberg took the helm as CEO and began a gradual transformation of the company. Among other steps, he gave greater decision-making authority to franchisees and field managers and slashed headquarters staff by 23 percent.

The changes most interesting for this case study, however, are those that occurred in the manufacturing and customer service processes in the restaurants. The McDonald's kitchen was revamped to include a computerized system to forecast customer traffic patterns and an assembly line to keep lettuce cold and burgers hot. This was done to ensure that food did not have to be kept in warming bins that degraded its taste. Moreover, processes were improved to make custom orders as simple as those at Burger King. These changes were fully implemented by the end of 1999.

Another change of some significance for Manufacturing was that the company changed its focus from big-bang initiatives that had flopped—like pizza, the Arch Deluxe, and the confusing "Campaign 55" discount—to getting the small things right in the restaurants.

Part of the philosophy of the McDonald's transformation under Greenberg is that the company's Procurement and Manufacturing functions need to be repositioned more effectively in the Compete quadrant so that their operating strategy coincides more closely with the corporate strategy. The stock market seems to have taken notice, too. The company's stock price rose 67 percent between February 1998 and February 1999, a growth rate that was three times that of the S&P 500 over that time.

The McDonald's case shows how a company can benefit by changing the role that the Procurement and Manufacturing groups play from their traditional role—focused exclusively on the Control quadrant—to one that is more closely aligned with market signals and the corporate strategy. Indeed, one of the messages of the case is that Procurement and Manufacturing can and should also play a role in shaping the strategy so that it is integrated with the company's strengths in those areas.

■ What Is Your Personal Measure of Success?

As Tables 4.1 and 4.2 indicate, the corporate measures of performance for the Procurement and Manufacturing functions do not always generate the appropriate incentives for maximizing value creation. This makes it particularly important for those involved in these functions to have personal measures of success that focus on value creation rather than just the on performance metrics for these functions.

An illustration of this point is the Procurement function of a company I worked with a few years ago. Like many others, this company assessed the performance of its Procurement function based on how well it managed the prices of raw material inputs and parts and components it purchased. Consequently, Procurement became very aggressive with its suppliers during price negotiations. This approach was successful in getting the company price concessions. Unfortunately, the suppliers began to view their relationship with the firm as purely that of vendors rather than business partners. The unintended consequence was that suppliers were discouraged from investing sufficiently in quality or feature improvements and innovations.

In the meantime, one of the major competitors of this company had taken the approach of developing strategic relationships with a few of its suppliers. It also focused on rewarding its suppliers for quality and feature improvements. While it was not lax in its price negotiations, it was willing to judiciously trade off price against quality of raw materials or feature innovations in parts and components—thereby gaining advantages that enabled it to significantly enhance the appeal of its products to customers. Moreover, it invited its suppliers to play a meaningful role in its own product innovation process by seeking their input at early stages of product development. In fact, in some cases, representatives of suppliers were on the company's new product development teams. Over time this company was able to sell its products at higher price points than the first company and gain a substantial competitive edge.

In the case of the first company, it would be unfair to put the entire blame for the erosion in the company's competitive position on the Procurement function. The primary culprit was probably the performance assessment system that created the wrong incentives for Procurement in the first place. Nevertheless, the effect was compounded by the fact that those in Procurement did not have their own definition of value creation that made the development of meaningful partnerships with suppliers a strategic priority.

Numerous companies make this mistake. Because of their strong Control quadrant positioning, they expect their Procurement functions to obtain price concessions from suppliers no matter what damage may be done to the strategic partnership. In fact, they often do not understand the very concept of a strategic partnership and the value it can produce. In a pure vendor relationship, the supplier simply provides the firm with what it asks for at the lowest possible cost. It does not make any investments in innovations or improvements that are not part of its legal contractual obligation. In contrast, in a strategic partnership the supplier and the firm work together as a team to work out the best solutions. Often the result is that the supplier makes investments in the relationship that it normally would not make.

Such a relationship can be an engine for innovation and unexpected value-creating product improvements.

■ Developing Speed

The importance of speed in manufacturing is well recognized in this era of time-based competition. Of course, gaining speed requires a manufacturing strategy that focuses on speed. The following case study is a nice example of how a company can design its manufacturing strategy for speed.

Building for Speed: Wabash National

With a 1999 market capitalization of about $500 million, Wabash National is a publicly traded company located in Lafayette, Indiana. It manufactures standard and customized truck trailers, including dry freight vans, refrigerated trailers, and bimodal vehicles. The company is the exclusive manufacturer of RoadRailer trailers, a patented bimodal technology owned by the company, which consists of trailers and detachable rail bogies that permit a vehicle to run both over the highway and directly on railroad lines. Wabash markets its products directly and through dealers to truckload and less-than-truckload common carriers, household moving and storage companies, leasing companies, and intermodal carriers.

The company boasts a world-class flexible manufacturing facility that requires very little changeover time to go from manufacturing a particular product to something else. The plant's design facilitates a high degree of customization and market responsiveness.

The company works closely with its product designers and its raw materials and component parts vendors. In fact, very little product design and engineering is done within the company. Much of it is outsourced. The company has developed durable relationships with independent product design engineers in the area who work for it on a freelance basis. Whenever they come up with a new product idea that they think the company could use, they offer it for sale to the company.

This approach has three important advantages. First, it allows Wabash National to free itself of having to own these assets, which increases its operating flexibility.

Second, the independent product design engineers typically have innovation and risk-taking incentives much stronger than those that employees of the company would have. The reason is that the independent engineers are sole owners of their ideas, which gives them high-powered market incentives. Employees of Wabash National, or any company for that matter, have *organizational incentives* that are typically not as high-powered, due to the problems of self-interested behavior discussed earlier.[4] This means that Wabash National can usually get to market faster with new products than a company that relies solely on its in-house talent for innovation. (Another example of this point is the entry of IBM into the personal computer market. Because IBM had fallen behind Apple in this market, speed of product development was essential. IBM achieved the necessary speed by outsourcing the operating system to Microsoft, the microprocessor to Intel, and the development of the software to a host of vendors.)

The third advantage of this approach is that it allows Wabash National to avoid the "not-invented-here" syndrome. Since those responsible for new product design are not housed within the firm, the company is less likely to pass up valuable outsourcing opportunities in manufacturing.

Wabash National also works closely with vendors who supply parts and components. It frequently involves them in the manufacturing process and develops deep relationships with them. This strategic partnership enhances vendors' ability to improve the quality and functionality of what they supply.

The final piece of the puzzle is employee training. Wabash National prides itself on its training. Not only are employees in the Manufacturing group well trained technically, but each of them is required to go through basic training in Finance and Accounting, so that they understand the entire value chain and the role of Manufacturing in it.

■ Organizational Success Strategies for Procurement and Manufacturing

Based on the content and case studies in this chapter, you can put together a model for success that can help move the Procurement and Manufacturing functions in an organization from their traditional Control quadrant position to one that permits more of a well-rounded focus on value creation (see Figure 4.1). This model is summarized in Figure 4.2.

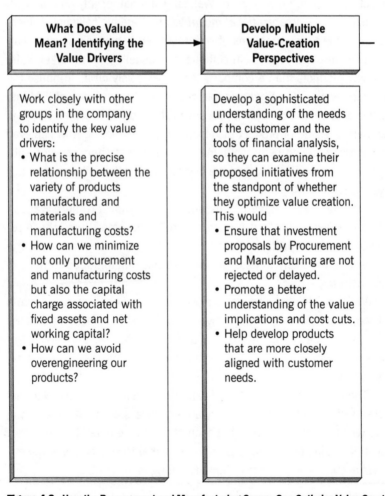

What Does Value Mean? Identifying the Value Drivers

Develop Multiple Value-Creation Perspectives

Work closely with other groups in the company to identify the key value drivers:
• What is the precise relationship between the variety of products manufactured and materials and manufacturing costs?
• How can we minimize not only procurement and manufacturing costs but also the capital charge associated with fixed assets and net working capital?
• How can we avoid overengineering our products?

Develop a sophisticated understanding of the needs of the customer and the tools of financial analysis, so they can examine their proposed initiatives from the standpont of whether they optimize value creation. This would
• Ensure that investment proposals by Procurement and Manufacturing are not rejected or delayed.
• Promote a better understanding of the value implications and cost cuts.
• Help develop products that are more closely aligned with customer needs.

Figure 4.2. How the Procurement and Manufacturing Groups Can Optimize Value Creation

The figure summarizes an expanded role for Procurement and Manufacturing that takes these functions outside their traditional Control quadrant domain and builds a greater awareness of market signals, shareholder value, and customer needs.

There are three main points to remember from this summary:

- The transactional currency of the Procurement and Manufacturing functions derives from the Control quadrant. This should focus these groups on seeking to minimize risk and

Develop Appropriate Strategy and Measures of Success	Organize for Speed
• Build a well-communicated strategy that is aligned with the overall corporate strategy. • Develop deep relationships and partnerships with vendors, not transactional relationships focused primarily on cost minimization. • Benchmark outsourcing options constantly to ensure that decisions optimize the value created for the whole firm. • Base outsourcing decisions on product development and manufacturing cycle times as well as direct cost comparisons.	• Establish open lines of communication with other parts of the organization to create an ongoing dialog about problems, solutions, and initiatives. • Have representatives serve on new product design teams to speed up emergence of new products along with representatives of key suppliers. • Use flexible manufacturing and strategic partnerships with suppliers to improve speed.

controlling costs, but it sometimes leads to behavior that overutilizes capital and suboptimizes value creation.

- Procurement and Manufacturing do not always communicate well with other functions. This can result in unwanted product variety and overinvestment in capital.
- Outsourcing and developing durable relationships with a limited number of suppliers or vendors are still underutilized tools for improving speed and optimizing value creation in Procurement and Manufacturing.

■ Personal Success Strategies for Procurement and Manufacturing

At the personal level, individuals within Procurement and Manufacturing should understand these points. First, the principles of personal success developed in the earlier chapters are applicable here as well. You must discover your own personal definition of value and your personal measures of success that help to distinguish you from others in the organization.

Second, Procurement and Manufacturing will always have a strong Control quadrant focus. So your personal definition of value, your strategy, and your personal measures of success must all be strong in the activities of this quadrant. For example, an important implication of being in the Control quadrant is that activities that expose the organization to risk should be avoided. This means Procurement should *always hedge* the prices of raw materials, components, and any outsourced parts. The ambivalence sometimes expressed by organizations on this issue—to hedge or not to hedge—is unnecessary. Trying to guess the future direction of prices is both dangerous and unwise. A significant part of your personal contribution to the organization should be to help reduce risk.

Similarly, Manufacturing is well advised to minimize risk in manufacturing processes through the use of Statistical Process

Control (SPC) techniques that are an integral part of Total Quality Management.[5] SPC helps you effectively manage (and minimize) the inherent variation in manufacturing processes. Companies such as Motorola have developed a strong reputation for deploying SPC to improve both the quality and predictability of their manufacturing. Other companies such as General Electric and Whirlpool have recently followed suit and integrated SPC techniques into their manufacturing operations. Becoming expert in these techniques should be a part of your personal development plan.

Third, it is important to identify what you can personally do to develop multiple value-creation perspectives and improve speed so that you can help move your organization to a more well-rounded view of value creation. The Wholonics model helps direct your activities here. As someone with a strong Control quadrant orientation, the "enemies" you need to get to know well are those in the diagonally opposite quadrant, which is Create. This means making friends with those in Marketing, Sales, and New Product Development. Understand what makes them tick. Learn about *their* performance metrics, how they define value, how they generate new ideas, what gets them excited. The most significant transformational moments, both for organizations and individuals, occur when opposites blend together.

CHAPTER SUMMARY

In this chapter the focus has been on how you can use the five secrets developed in the opening chapters to become a better value creator in Procurement and Manufacturing. A survey of these functions indicates that the Control quadrant of the Wholonics model dominates the meaning of value creation as well as the measures of value in these functions. This potentially leads to three kinds of impediments to developing the appropriate multiple value-creation perspectives: (1) a "manufacturing is king" mind-set that leads to overinvestment at the expense of value creation, (2) poor product decisions that lead to overengineered products with insufficient innovation and outsourcing, and (3) lack of effective communication with other parts of the organization, leading to the manufacturing of products that don't always match up well with what customers would like. The solution is for Procurement and Manufacturing to reposition themselves more in the Compete, Create, and Collaborate quadrants, and for individuals to have personal measures of success that focus them on value creation even when the corporate performance metrics don't.

It is important for a company to integrate its manufacturing strategy with its overall strategy and also to make sure that Procurement and Manufacturing have a role to play in shaping corporate strategy. The Wabash National case study illustrated how Procurement and Manufacturing can develop a strategy that focuses on speed, thereby giving a company an important advantage in this age of time-based competition. To convert this advantage into a privileged relationship with the customer requires value creation to be well understood by those in Marketing, Sales and Distribution, and New Product Development, the topic of the next chapter.

Reflections and Discussion

Organizational Steps for Improving
Value Creation in Procurement and Manufacturing

1. Conduct a survey of those in your Procurement and Manufacturing organizations to construct the analogs of Table 4.1 and Table 4.2 for your company. Summarize the lessons that you learn from the survey about how these functions view value creation and the effectiveness of the performance metrics being used for these functions. Develop an action plan to deal with these lessons.

2. Write your Procurement strategy and your Manufacturing strategy, each in three bullet points or less. Write a brief paragraph describing how each strategy is consistent with your overall corporate strategy. Be sure to (a) identify the key value drivers to which each strategy is linked and (b) specify the manner in which these strategies take a multiple-value-creation-perspectives approach that will position Procurement and Manufacturing more in the Compete and Create quadrants.

3. What distinguishes your Procurement and Manufacturing strategies from those of your competitors? How do these strategies create a sustainable competitive advantage for your organization?

4. What performance metrics do you have for measuring and rewarding speed in Procurement and Manufacturing? How do you compare to your competitors on the dimension of speed?

Personal Steps for Improving
Value Creation in Procurement and Manufacturing

1. Write down the ten most important activities you engage in and identify which quadrant each activity predominantly belongs to. Use your list to draw a Wholonics profile based on this. Then draw a desired Wholonics profile for yourself and identify at least three new activities you will have to engage in to help move you to the desired profile. Since the total amount of time available is the same as before, you will have to determine which of the ten activities you previously engaged in will be allocated less of your time now. Include in these activities at least one that involves getting to make new friends and the names of those from Marketing, Sales, and New Product Development you will get to know better.

2. Write down a brief personal statement of strategy that will produce actions on your part that will move you to your desired Wholonics profile. Make sure it is consistent with the three new activities identified in step 1. Also write a brief paragraph describing how your strategy will distinguish you from others in your organization.

3. Write down your personal measures of success, at least one of which differs from what your organization defines as performance assessment metrics for you. Ask yourself how your personal measures of success help you to overcome sunflower management.

4. Do you get tasks accomplished at a rate that surpasses others in your organization? Is your ability to do this improving through time? Develop an action plan to improve your speed, including parallel processing of multiple tasks.

Improving
Value Creation
in Marketing, Sales and
Distribution, and New
Product Development

Companies in retail-oriented business often live or die on the basis of their marketing efforts. For example, in the past Coca-Cola used to regularly beat PepsiCo in the race for market share because of its tremendous brand equity. However, under CEO Roger A. Enrico, who took the helm in 1996, PepsiCo launched a reinvigorated marketing campaign that put enormous pressure on Coca-Cola to defend its 44–31 percent market share lead over Pepsi.[1] The campaign involved a doubling of Pepsi's marketing budget to $300 million per year.

While price and product quality are important to consumers of Coke and Pepsi, there is little doubt that demand is significantly driven by brand perceptions, effectiveness of distribution strategies, and the timeliness of marketing initiatives in connecting the product with high-visibility events like sporting playoffs or movie launches. In other industries, the effect of marketing may be less dramatic. But the fact remains that marketing is usually a potent tool for value creation. In light of this, it is critically important for individuals in Marketing, Sales and Distribution (S&D), and New Product Development to be great value creators.

There are countless opportunities for value creation in Marketing, S&D, and New Product Development—opportunities that are often missed. In this chapter you will see how you can use the five keys to value creation make your fullest contribution to value creation in these areas.

■ What Does Value Mean to You and Your Organization?

A few years ago a company I was working with decided to develop a new product based on market research data. This product was a significant improvement over existing offerings in the market from both cost and quality standpoints. Since the product could not be manufactured in any of the company's existing plants, management decided to build a new one.

The decision to build a new plant was made after careful financial analysis that revealed that the multimillion-dollar investment in property, plant, and equipment would have a positive Net Present Value (NPV). Embedded in the financial analysis were assumptions about the prices at which the various models of the new product would be sold.

The plant opened its doors, slightly behind schedule. But everything else was on target. At the end of the first year, the plant manager had every reason to be pleased. The plant was running at full capacity and product demand was high. In fact, the plant had a hard time keeping up with demand.

The company then decided to do a routine post-audit of the financial performance of its very large investment. To the shock and dismay of many, it was discovered that, on a *forward-looking basis,* the plant investment had a negative NPV if the status quo was maintained. How could this be?

Upon closer inspection, the problem surfaced. Almost every variable was according to the numbers that had gone into the financial analysis supporting the initial capital request, except one: price! It turned out that the prices that were being charged for the various stock keeping units (SKUs) being produced were lower than those assumed in the capital allocation request. When the person responsible for the post-audit looked into why, he was told by the S&D group that the prices were "market-determined." The market was unwilling to support the higher prices that had been assumed before the plant was built.

What was perplexing was that this was a situation in which demand seemed to exceed available supply. The basic lesson of Economics 101 is that in such a case you should raise price, even though doing so is likely to lower the quantity of demand. Unfortunately, the S&D group had not experimented with higher prices and was unwilling to do so even when informed about the negative NPV. So this company kept churning out unit after unit of various types of the new product, and each unit destroyed the company's shareholder value!

Why did this company behave in this manner? The answer lies in two organizational realities. First, in many companies, the assumptions that go into the budgeting analysis that supports a capital request are often disconnected from what happens after the capital is received and the project is launched. All too often those who do the initial financial analysis—the Finance group— are not those who make the pricing decisions after the product is launched. They solicit data inputs from those in Marketing and S&D, but they really have no price-decision authority. Once the product is launched, the Marketing and S&D groups don't feel compelled to abide by what Finance regarded as promises made in the capital allocation request. Their decisions are driven by what they view as the realities of the marketplace.

Second, in this case, there was a problem with the way the S&D group defined value. This group perceived value creation as increasing market share. After all, wasn't that the whole rationale for launching the new product? Who knows what increasing price would do to sales and market share? Perhaps the only indisputable fact was that these would not go up! So the decision was made to not raise price and risk lowering sales and market share, even though raising the prices might have created more value.

Table 5.1 reports large-sample survey results about the pervasiveness of these problems, particularly as they relate to how those in Marketing, S&D, and New Product Development define value.

One of the first things that struck me when I looked at these results was how much more information I seemed to have with this group than with other functional areas. To me this was an indication that the tensions and the number of unresolved issues were greater. A few other interesting facts emerged as well.

First, the typical performance metrics are narrowly focused on the Marketing functional silo rather than on overall value creation. Moreover, these metrics don't correspond very well to the value drivers that the members of these groups perceived to be important. (Compare the first two columns in Table 5.1.) However, the difference between the two was not as large as one would imagine based on the level of frustration reflected in how much their managers viewed the financial goals of the company as impeding value creation. One possible explanation is that there are budgetary and other financial constraints these groups face that are not reflected in the explicit performance metrics listed in the table. Every organization is governed by both explicit and implicit rules. Perhaps the constraints that frustrate

Table 9.1. The role of marketing, sales and distribution and how Product perception in value creation

What performance metrics do you typically use?	How does your group create value? What are the value drivers you control?	How do you destroy value?	How do the financial goals of the company impede your value creation?	How would you like to redefine these goals?
■ Revenue growth ■ Market share ■ Successful new-product launches ■ Achieve sales targets ■ Meeting deliverables within time and budget ■ Cost control ■ Profitability ■ Brand management	■ Brand development ■ People development ■ Growth in existing and new markets ■ Increasing sales ■ Increasing profits ■ Increasing customer satisfaction ■ Developing new e-commerce products	■ Developing products that do not meet market needs ■ Creating nonstandard local solutions for global needs ■ Pricing products based on resources allocated to the product rather than market demand ■ Continuing with sales of unprofitable products ■ Poor new product introduction ■ Poor management of marketing and promotion strategies ■ Bureaucratic and inefficient organization structures ■ Poor change management with respect to product pricing	■ Pressures to optimize inventories and reduce SKU complexity ■ Internal operating profit and EVA turn-around goals that create short-term financial pressure ■ Constraints on resources to engineer products and increase product quality ■ Lack of investment that delays new-product launches ■ Pressure to reduce headcount and increase prices ■ Lack of investment for R&D	■ Judge employees on customer satisfaction ■ Invest for long-term potential and judge people on how well they develop brand strength ■ Strike the right balance between margins and revenues ■ Replace cost cutting with cost management and put more emphasis on investment rather than cost ■ Empower middle management to reinvest in product lines

Marketing and affiliated groups are those emanating from having to meet tighter budget constraints than they view as optimal from a value-creation standpoint.

Second, there seems to be considerable confusion about the distinction between value drivers and outcomes. Many of the items listed under value drivers, such as increasing sales, profits, and customer satisfaction, are really outcomes. Thus, the basic understanding of *how* to create value seems fuzzy.

Third, many of the impediments that members of these groups perceive as arising from the financial goals of the company have to do with constraints on resources, both financial and human, and pressure to optimize the use of capital by reducing SKU complexity or cutting back on investments in product development. Resource constraints are a recurring theme in various functional areas and thus not surprising; recall the discussion in the previous chapter. It is interesting, though, that while these groups viewed the reduction of SKU complexity as a value destroyer, the Manufacturing groups did not refer to it at all (refer to Table 4.1). This suggests that the directive to reduce SKU complexity has its origins in a part of the organization other than Manufacturing.

Fourth, there are surprising similarities in the value destroyers identified by these groups and those identified by Manufacturing in Table 4.2—in particular, developing products that do not meet market needs, poor new product introduction, and bureaucratic and inefficient organization.

Finally, it is also striking that, like the people in Manufacturing, those in Marketing, S&D, and New Product Development view the financial goals of the company as being overly short term in their orientation. All these groups seem to be starved for a more long-term view from senior management and for greater empowerment in managing their value creation activities.

This viewpoint, while compelling in some respects, also suggests a serious lack of communication about value creation. One of the things that led Japanese and Korean firms astray was taking too long term a perspective. After all, as John Maynard Keynes once observed, "In the long run, we are all dead!" Knowing how to strike the appropriate balance between the short term and the long term and then effectively communicating the decision-making ramifications of this balance is one of the keys to resolving these tensions.

The survey results also provide examples of other impediments to a shared understanding of value. Examples of self-interested behavior and the negative zone of competition include creating nonstandard local solutions for global needs and continuing with sales of unprofitable products. Examples of a functional silo mentality include developing products that do not meet market needs and poor change management with respect to product pricing.

■ Multiple Value-Creation Perspectives

Traditionally, Marketing and its affiliated groups have operated in the Create quadrant of the Wholonics model. This sometimes makes it difficult for these groups to take a more holistic approach to value creation. There are four problems that stand in the way: the "can't make money without marketing" syndrome, fascination with a geographic rather than brand or product focus, reluctance to cannibalize existing products, and an exclusive focus on product that ignores innovations in Sales and Distribution.

The "Can't Make Money Without Marketing" Syndrome

It is hard to find a marketing person in a company who believes that the Marketing Department budget is high enough to meet the company's strategic goals. The prevailing viewpoint that marketing budgets are insufficient has been reinforced by the explosion of marketing spending by e-commerce companies, as the following case study indicates.

Marketing Expenses and the Internet

It is well known that the enormous amount of money being spent on marketing by Internet companies is one of the reasons few of these companies have so far turned a profit. As one observer remarked, "It's a time when losing money can be a badge of success, while making money can be a sign of lack of imagination."[2]

The reason for these large marketing outlays is clear: gaining market share and developing loyal customers is essential to the viability and future success of Internet companies. This is, of course, true in any industry. But this truth is magnified many times over for Internet companies because of the extraordinarily low barriers to entry and the minuscule marginal cost of providing services over the Web. Thus, marketing is the path to achieving market dominance, which then means long-run success.

The Internet marketing model is the stuff dreams are made of for anybody involved in the marketing function anywhere. It addresses many of the frustrations summarized in Table 5.1 since it indicates a willingness to invest in the long-term future of the company without worrying about short-term profits.

But what is the financial justification for devoting all these resources to marketing? More marketing may be better than less at certain levels of marketing expenditure, but surely that can't be true at all levels. So how much is enough?

It is difficult to know the answer based on studying Internet companies. Their high stock market valuations provide them with what is perceived to be easy access to capital, which then provides resources for large marketing outlays. Are they spending what they believe they can afford or is the spending based on a financial model that says that the marketing investment has a positive NPV?

I don't know the answer to this question, but I am reminded of a conversation with the CFO of a company that had invited me to assist in developing a resource allocation system for evaluating investment proposals. I asked the CFO whether marketing expenditures were to be included as part of these process. His reply reflected what I believe is the norm at many companies: "No. They'd never allow us to include marketing outlays in this process. Besides, we have no idea how to even go about doing an NPV analysis on marketing expenditures. We'll just set marketing budgets based on what we spent last year and our sales growth targets for this year."

There is no doubt that evaluating the benefits of marketing outlays is viewed by organizations as more difficult than evaluating other types of capital investments, perhaps because marketing's benefits are harder to measure. But any resource allocation analysis involves forecasting future cash flows. These forecasts are often educated guesses—and there is no reason why they cannot be done for marketing outlays. At the very least, you would learn how large the future benefits would have to be to justify the marketing investments. Having the Internet mind-set that more marketing spending must mean greater value creation is not a substitute for careful financial analysis that could force decision makers to confront key assumptions and justify their reasonableness.[3]

Short of such careful financial scrutiny, one could at least look at somewhat crude but revealing measures like the ratio of revenues to marketing expenses. The idea is that the winners in the marketing sweepstakes are likely to be those who can generate the highest values for this ratio. Those who cannot generate sufficient incremental revenues by their marketing spending are not getting sufficient return on their marketing investment and may be unable to sustain such investment. *Business Week* computed this ratio for Internet companies and found significant differences in marketing efficiency across companies, as shown in Table 5.2.

Table 5.2. Ratios of Revenues to Marketing Expenses for Selected Internet Companies

Company	Ratio 1997	Ratio 1998	Percent Change From 1997 to 1998
Onsale	9.69	8.81	−9
America Online	3.99	6.95	74
Amazon.com	3.65	4.59	26
E*Trade	5.55	3.44	−38
TheGlobe.com	0.62	0.59	−4
iVillage	0.69	0.53	−23
TheStreet.com	0.27	0.46	70

Source: Debra Sparks, "Who's Getting More Bang for the Marketing Buck," *Business Week* (May 31, 1999): 148–150.

For the firms *Business Week* looked at, the average ratio was 3.37 for 1997 and 2.70 for 1998. This suggests a couple of points. First, in the increasingly crowded world of e-commerce, there *may* be diminishing returns to scale in the impact of marketing on revenues. (I emphasize "may" because it would be foolish to put much weight on any statistical inference based on comparing just two numbers.) Second, there is considerable variance in the revenue-to-marketing expense ratio across these companies, with some companies realizing surprisingly low ratios.[4] It is possible that at least some of these companies are making negative NPV marketing investments.

One way to think about this is as follows. Suppose that each of the companies in Table 5.2 will someday be like Microsoft—a heroic assumption indeed. Then Microsoft's 1997 data will support some interesting conjectures. In 1997, Microsoft earned $11.358 billion in revenues and generated $4.689 billion in positive cash flow from operations. This gives a ratio of cash flow to revenue of 0.4128. You compute cash flow in this sort of situation because ultimately that is what investors want, not revenues. Suppose you further assume that $1 in marketing spending will produce an *incremental* revenue in that time period for an Internet company that is half its actual revenue. (The assumption is that the other half is due to the reputation of the company's products and services due to the real value they provide consumers.) You then get the following formula for the NPV of that $1 spent in marketing:

$$NPV = \text{Revenue to Marketing Expense Ratio} \times 0.5 \times 0.4128 - \$1.$$

If you apply this formula to Onsale in 1998 you get:

$$NPV = 8.81 \times 0.5 \times 0.4128 - 1 = \$1.8184 - \$1 = \$0.8184$$

According to this approach, a company would need to have a revenue/market expenses ratio of about 4.85 before it can hope to create value with its marketing expenses. A lower ratio would mean that the marketing expense is not producing enough incremental revenue to make it worthwhile.

Of course, this approach is rather simplistic in that it ignores the fact that the marketing expenses in any given year may have cash flow implications that extend well into the future. The point, then, is not to take these numbers literally, but rather to note that marketing outlays need to be subjected to the rigors of financial analysis to see whether Economic Value is being created. One of the traditional weaknesses of Marketing is that such analyses are not done.

Fascination with a Geographic Rather Than a Brand or Product Focus

Because a deep knowledge of the customer is considered essential to marketing success and customers are assumed to vary from country to country in their preferences, companies often end up significantly balkanizing their Marketing and S&D groups. Each region of the world ends up with its own set of specialists. The company develops a geographic focus rather than a brand or product focus, and there is usually ineffective communication across geographies, including the development of expensive local solutions to global needs (see Table 5.1).

The solution is to move from a geographic focus to a product focus. This shift typically involves a significant reorganization of the firm—but it can pay off handsomely, as many firms like Unilever, Philips, and Procter & Gamble (P&G) have found.

Rejuvenating a Brand Family: Procter & Gamble

In 1998, P&G was mired in difficulty. It had declared in 1996 that it would double its net sales to $70 billion by 2006. Unfortunately, it had consistently missed its revenue growth target. Its much-publicized new products were experiencing disappointing sales, and the economic slowdown in foreign markets was hurting its prospects as well. Between July and October 1998, its stock price fell from $94 to $70.

After much introspection, the company decided it needed to become simpler and faster. It came up with a plan to fundamentally reorganize itself. The plan, called Organization 2005, would flatten the P&G hierarchy, install a new product development process to facilitate faster new-product introductions, and replace the existing geographic organization of the company with seven global business units organized by product category.[5]

These business units are responsible for developing and selling products on a global basis. This replaces the old system in which P&G's country managers were responsible for setting prices and managing the product mix in their regions. The new global business units are also charged with the responsibility for overseeing new product development.

Part of the reason for P&G reorganization is the pressures it faced from its largest global customers, such as Wal-Mart and the French mega-retailer Carrefour. With their own global expansion firmly under way, these retailers are most interested in *global sourcing,* which included paying a single price for a given product rather than having to negotiate with individual P&G organizations in different parts of the world. P&G's reorganization would be a step in the direction of realizing that goal. More generally, developing a brand and product focus that transcends geographical boundaries is often an essential step in developing the appropriate value-creation perspective.

Reluctance to Cannibalize Existing Product: The New Products Versus Old Products Dilemma

Companies typically have portfolios of old and new products. In considering whether to introduce a new product, there are three basic issues to be considered:

1. What is the market potential of this new product?
2. To what extent will this new product *cannibalize* my existing products?
3. If I don't introduce the new product, what is the probability that a competitor will? That is, how well can I defend the turf of my old product from competitive threats?

Marketing obviously has a major role to play in assessing the market potential of any new product. Where things get tricky is in estimating cannibalization. The higher the cannibalization estimate, the less attractive the new product looks. What complicates matters is that the relevance of cannibalization for the new-product introduction decision cannot be judged in isolation from the likelihood of competitive entry. The more likely a competitor is to enter and hurt your existing product, the more attractive the new product looks.

When Marketing groups make errors in judgment in this regard, the problem usually stems from underestimating the probability of competitive entry or overestimating the company's ability to defend its own turf with its existing products in case a competitor enters—or both. This type of miscalculation is very common, and leads to the introduction of fewer new products than would be the case if such estimation errors were not made.

Perhaps the best illustration of this point is what happened to the U.S. automobile industry in the 1970s and 1980s. During the 1960s and 1970s many U.S. carmakers had developed prototypes of fuel-efficient compact cars. They chose not to introduce these cars to the market because they were worried about cannibalizing their existing lines. In retrospect, it is clear that they underestimated the probability that the Japanese carmakers would successfully introduce these products anyway.

Thus, the decision-making flaws that corrupt the new-product introduction decision can be visualized as depicted Figure 5.1.

As the figure clarifies, the decision to introduce the new product is arrived at after multiplying two low probabilities (both possibly underestimated), which means it often ends up being a *very* low-probability event.

Why do companies make these errors? Part of the answer may have to do with the basic psychology of human behavior.

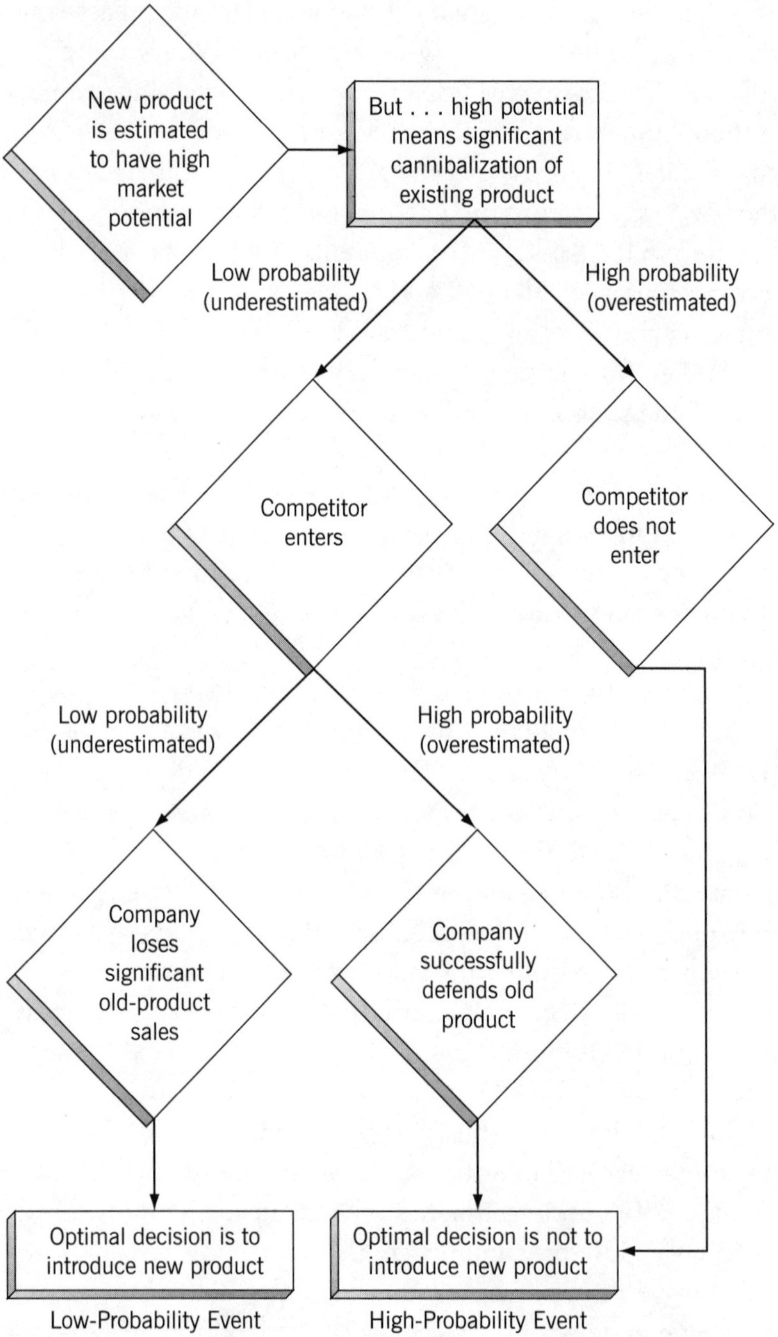

Figure 5.1. How Estimation Biases Lead to the Wrong New-Product Decision

Underestimating the probability of a competitor entering is linked to the well-known *overoptimism bias* in human behavior. This was incisively noted by the famous economist, John Maynard Keynes, who argued that overoptimism was the reason why so many people bought inadequate insurance against calamities like fire, floods, death, and so on. That is, most people tend to overestimate the probability of good things happening to them and underestimate the probability of misfortune. This bias may indeed be genetically hardwired to promote a feeling of well-being and good psychological health.

Overestimating the probability that the company will successfully defend its old product turf in the face of competition probably stems from the *overconfidence bias* in human behavior,[6] which causes people to overestimate the quality of their own information. Thus, a company that is inadequately informed about the magnitude of the competitive threat mistakenly believes that its market position is more secure than it really is.

Quite often, a company that is excellent in creating new product ideas is not very adept at defending the market position of its existing products. Why is this so? The reason is that generating new product ideas is a skill that belongs to the Create quadrant of the Wholonics model, whereas defending the market position of existing products is a skill that belongs to the Compete quadrant. Very often, the development of skills in one quadrant occurs at the expense of skills in another quadrant.

Every company needs to be competitive both in introducing new products and in defending its own turf against competitive assaults on existing products. The former requires Create quadrant competencies and the latter requires Compete quadrant competencies. Thus, once again it is necessary to develop multiple value-creation perspectives and competencies that span multiple quadrants of the Wholonics model.

Exclusive Focus on Product:
Ignoring Breakthroughs in Sales and Distribution

When companies think of becoming better at connecting with their customers, they typically focus on the attributes of the product and the creation of its brand image. As discussed earlier, a brand focus is often essential for success and is strongly preferable in the majority of cases to a geographic focus. But it could come at the expense of value-creation opportunities elsewhere. For example, there is often a propensity to ignore breakthroughs in S&D. Yet some of the most exciting new value-creation strategies have emanated from innovations in distribution channels.

Take the example of Avon. It pioneered a breakthrough in the way cosmetics were sold by shunning the usual retail distribution channel and developing the concept of door-to-door selling. By 1976, it was significantly outperforming its closest rival, Revlon, in almost every financial performance category. A more recent example similar to the Avon-Revlon battle is related in the following case study of Compaq versus Dell.

Head to Head in Computer Sales: Compaq Versus Dell

Computer giant Compaq made its mark by successfully reverse-engineering the IBM PC and then introducing a much cheaper competing product. The company steadily grew its market share, and by August 1995 it became the market leader in overall PC sales.

Compaq's distribution strategy, however, was based largely on selling through distributors like Ingram and Tech Data. That is, it used a predominantly traditional distribution strategy. And then came Dell Computer Corporation with its innovative build-to-order manufacturing system that allowed customers to order directly from Dell—either by phone or online—and have a customized PC delivered to their home. By 1999, Dell could deliver a PC in about three days from the time of order compared to twelve days for Compaq, and was selling over $10 million worth of PCs per day.

Dell's strategy allowed it to win corporate customers away from Compaq, but that is only part of the story. Dell's unique manufacturing and distribution system allowed it to minimize inventories. Keeping inventories down was much more difficult for Compaq, which was still building to forecasts from retailers. The consequence of all this is that even though Compaq was twice as large as Dell in revenues, its market capitalization was only about 40 percent of that of Dell.

It is not as if Compaq was unaware of its competitive handicap in its core PC business. It remained, after all, an outstanding company in many other businesses, including storage systems and PCs in the below-$600 price range. However, the company appeared to face two obstacles in competing with Dell. First, its build-to-order manufacturing system was not nearly up to par with Dell's. Second, trying to sell PCs direct to customers created "channel conflict," putting it in competition with its own retail distributors. This is a nasty problem. For example, when Compaq announced in September 1998 that the Prosignia line for small businesses would be available only on its Web site and not through retail distributors, its distributors complained about being excluded. Eventually, Compaq reversed course.[7]

Incidentally, this problem is not unique to Compaq. In the appliance industry, for example, manufacturers like General Electric, Maytag, and Whirlpool have long been aware of the power of mega-retailers like Sears and Wal-Mart, as well as the benefits to the manufacturer of going directly to the consumer. But a major impediment to going direct is that doing so would incur the wrath of the mega-retailers who are appliance distributors and with whom the manufacturers would now be competing directly.

The major lesson of this case study is that enormous value-creation opportunities may be lost when the business design of a company has a redundant layer of intermediation between itself and the end customer. However, once you are trapped in such a business design, it may be difficult to escape to a better future without destroying the present.

The challenge then for Marketing and affiliated groups is to overcome their strong Create quadrant orientation and let decisions be guided by other value-creation perspectives that exist within the organization. Unfortunately, the survey results in Table 5.2 indicate that some of the Compete quadrant considerations are viewed as value destroyers by Marketing. Clearly, these perceptions must be corrected as you seek to evolve your Wholonics profile along lines depicted in Figure 5.2.

What this diagram shows is that Marketing should divert greater resources to being more focused on the shareholder-value aspects of the Compete quadrant and the way Marketing decisions impact shareholder value. This can often be done through effective education and training programs for managers that include decision-making simulations.

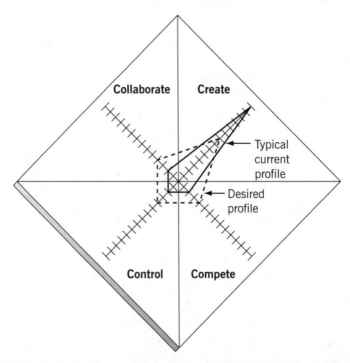

Figure 5.2. The Desired Evolution of Marketing and Affiliated Groups in the Wholonics Perspective

■ What Is Your Business Strategy?

As with any group, the overall corporate strategy must determine the strategy of Marketing and its affiliated groups. A great example of how corporate strategy can drive changes in both the strategy and organization of Marketing and related groups is provided by a case study of Citibank.

Banking for the World: Citibank

By 1997, Citibank was one of the most profitable U.S. banks and perhaps the most global.[8] It provided a full range of financial services for corporate customers with the exception of investment banking in the United States. Its two main businesses were corporate banking and consumer banking.

This was a dramatic change from the beginning of the decade. In 1990 and 1991, Citibank was in dire straits—its stock price hovered around $8 and there were rumors that the bank would be closed. The crisis resulted from an inefficient cost structure and credit risk management problems that manifested themselves in disastrous losses in real estate lending. By 1994 Citibank had revamped its credit risk management process and gotten its cost structure under control. With its financial health restored, the bank turned to its overall strategy and organization.

Citibank's strategy was guided by the goal of expanding the bank's "share of its customers' minds." This meant developing detailed knowledge of customer demands, both across geographies and products, so as to deepen customer relationships and improve Citibank's competitive standing.

The bank viewed its own structure as an integral component of executing its strategy. Prior to the mid-1990s, its corporate banking business in the developed (OECD) countries was organized along geographic lines. Country managers had almost complete autonomy in decision making, resource allocation, and performance evaluation. Each country unit had its own product specialists and customer relationship managers, who were responsible for direct relationships with customers headquartered in that country.

In addition, the bank had the World Corporate Group (WCG) to serve approximately two hundred multinational corporate customers. The WCG was intended to be a customer-oriented overlay to the geography-based organization of corporate banking. However, the WCG commanded no resources. Rather, WCG managers had to appeal to the country managers for resources to serve their corporate customers. For example, if the WCG needed product specialists to serve some customers, they would have to request the relevant country managers to release them.

In 1994 Citibank concluded that this organizational structure was not the best way to execute its strategy. It reorganized its corporate banking business in 1995 by establishing its Global Relationship Bank (GRB) to serve corporate customers in the OECD countries and its Emerging Markets unit to serve corporate customers in other countries. The GRB was organized along product, geography, and customer dimensions at the same time. Most customers were grouped into one of fourteen industry categories. To strengthen the GRB's focus on customer relationships, the customer dimension was given the highest priority and the geography dimension the lowest priority. Thus, the creation of the GRB deemphasized geography. The idea was to increase cooperation among Product, Geography, and Relationship managers. Performance incentives, including the variable compensation system, were revamped to reward employees for strengthening customer relationships and "winning a larger share of the customer's wallet."

These changes were successful in moving corporate banking away from geography and toward customers. Relationship managers focused more on deepening customer relationships and identifying opportunities for selling new products and services. And Product managers paid increasing attention to designing products that met customer demands and to making Relationship managers aware of these products.

Citibank's Emerging Markets unit was organized by geography, however. According to Citibank's management, they chose this pattern deliberately. "We focus on each local country. We then link the geographies tightly together as a single franchise, to promote success transfer, standard processing approaches, rapid product rollouts, and career development."[9]

Citibank typically began activities in an emerging market as a result of its dealings with the global customers served by the GRB. As financial markets in the country developed, Citibank broadened its business by acquiring local clients and introducing new products. Thus the Emerging Markets unit arose both from a desire to take advantage of higher profit margins in emerging markets and the desire to build the most extensive global network of any bank to support the GRB's strategy of serving OECD clients with global demands.

Interactions between the GRB and the Emerging Markets unit were informal, and there was no formal credit or compensation reward for cooperation.

Over the next two years, Citibank learned that although the new organization was an improvement over its predecessor, it was not entirely satisfactory. The GRB became so customer-focused that it began to ignore products—such as syndicated loans—that were not heavily demanded by customers. A second problem was the relationships with investors like mutual and hedge funds were not fully harvested. Finally, it was difficult to standardize services because of the separation of the GRB from the Emerging Markets unit. Often, separate product specialists from these two groups worked with the same customer.

To deal with this loss of product business and to improve standardization, Citibank again reorganized its corporate banking business in 1997. This created a new unit called Global Markets in which *all* product specialists were housed. This eliminated the artificial product boundary between the GRB and the Emerging Markets unit. The Global Markets unit was also charged with the responsibility to focus on relationships with investors to provide seamless transactions between issuers of securities, corporate customers, and investors in securities.

The Citibank case illustrates the changes that are often necessary to get an organization to become truly customer-focused and align corporate and Marketing strategies. Marketing can and should play an active role in initiating such changes. Since customer focus is an important activity of the Compete quadrant, this case illustrates once again the importance of the Compete quadrant for Marketing and affiliated groups. But since Citibank's initiatives also resulted in a reorganization, it also required Collaborate quadrant competencies.

Another good example of how corporate strategy defines an effective Marketing and New Product Development strategy is provided by a case study of EMC.

Strategy-Driven Marketing: EMC

EMC is a highly successful company in the computer industry. It makes data storage products and enjoys a P/E ratio of 65 to 70.

In 1999 the CEO of EMC was Michael C. Ruettgers. When he became CEO in 1992, EMC's profits were $30 million. Sales were $386 million, and profit margins were around 6–7 percent. Forecasts for year-end 1999 were $1 billion in profits, $5.3 billion in sales, and 20 percent in profit margins. From March 1998 to March 1999, EMC shareholders earned a staggering return of 167 percent, eclipsing even companies like Microsoft, Intel, Cisco, and Dell. The company had achieved a 35 percent market share in industrial-strength storage systems. Its customers included the top twenty telecommunication companies, 90 percent of the world's major airlines, and the twenty-five largest U.S. banks.[10]

How did Ruettgers achieve such success? The simple answer is that he displayed a remarkable capacity for excelling in both the Create and Compete quadrants of the Wholonics model. In particular, he showed

- An acute awareness of the importance of product quality and customer satisfaction and the willingness to commit significant organizational resources to guarantee quality and customer satisfaction
- An ability to gather valuable new-product ideas by talking to customers
- The willingness to abandon proven but mature markets in pursuit of untested but potentially promising new markets

The first two attributes are principally from the Compete quadrant, whereas the third is often the key to success in the Create quadrant. To show the first attribute at work, I must go all the way back to 1989 when Ruettgers was in his first year as head of operations and customer service at EMC. The company was confronted with a crisis related to quality problems. Its data-storage equipment was crashing because its engineers had failed to detect faulty disk drives supplied by NEC Corporation. In response to this problem, Ruettgers decided to offer customers replacements of faulty parts or entire new systems. The company ended up spending $100 million in less than a year. It also hired engineers who were specialists in locating the flaw that haunted the company. They tore apart the drives to find the flaw. Ruettgers also instituted rigorous new quality controls. To help keep the company solvent, senior managers accepted a 20 percent salary cut.

Eventually, the company solved its quality problems and was back on track by 1990. Ruettgers, now EMC president, turned his attention to developing world-class products. Through conversations with his customers he realized that most companies use only 20 percent of their stored data for most of their daily operations. He thus ordered cancellation of nine major product lines, amounting to 80 percent of revenues, so as to focus resources on developing a super-fast storage system that companies could use for ready access to their most important information. This product would put EMC in direct competition with IBM mainframes.

Within six months of introducing the product, EMC had managed to convince many of IBM's mainframe customers to switch over from IBM's giant memory devices to EMC's less expensive product, made up of disk drives linked together. Three years later, EMC had replaced IBM as the leading supplier of storage for IBM's own mainframes. By 1992, Ruettgers was appointed CEO of EMC.

Ruettgers did not sit still. While talking to a John Deere data center manager, he came to appreciate a major problem facing customers like this one. Many companies had invested millions of dollars in new computer networks, but the new servers were not as reliable as mainframes; they crashed more often. Consequently, there was a lot of important information that now was scattered across many different machines that did not "talk to each other." Ruettgers's epiphany was in visualizing a single storage system that could hold data from many different computers.

The problem with the new idea was that it would cannibalize the product with which EMC had replaced IBM as the leader in data storage systems. That product was yielding EMC handsome returns and was expected to grow at 20 percent for at least two more years. Over the objections of many senior executives, Ruettgers decided to go ahead with the new product—Symmetrix "open storage" systems.

Although the early results were not encouraging, eventually Symmetrix was a big hit. The system was so versatile that EMC was able to charge premium prices. By 1998, open storage systems accounted for over $2 billion in revenues.

EMC's success clearly illustrates three important principles of operating in the Create quadrant. First, not only should you not worry too much about cannibalizing your existing products, you should actively seek to cannibalize them. It is a fast-moving, competitive world. Any new product idea you have that you don't pursue is conceding potentially valuable turf to your competitors. As someone once remarked, "In the new product introduction game, I'd rather cannibalize than be eaten up by others. With cannibalization, I can at least choose which body part to munch on."

Second, although risk is something to be minimized in the Control and Compete quadrants, it often has to be embraced in the Create quadrant. Abandoning an existing product that was expected to grow at 20 percent in favor of an untried new product was *not* a low-risk strategy for EMC. But while such risk taking seems excessive from a short-run perspective, it may be necessary to take advantage of the long-run potential of the opportunity.

Third, conventional market research, which involves asking customers what they want, is far from the best way to generate new product ideas. There have been some spectacular product failures because of such market research. For example, McDonald's introduced the McLean burger because taste tests with consumers were very encouraging. And yet the product flopped. At the other extreme, Chrysler would never have introduced its minivan had it allowed itself to be influenced by initial customer surveys in which those who were shown concept drawings of the proposed minivan reacted negatively.

The reason why conventional market research fails is that customers are not always very good at providing useful feedback about products that have not been developed yet. As W. Edwards Deming once observed very astutely, one should never ask customers what they want or students what they should learn.

The better approach is to follow Ruettgers's lead and talk to customers about their problems. Every problem to which you can find a new solution is a new product! Among other companies that have used this approach successfully is the furniture maker Steelcase. The company assembles office products for its customers based on observations about how the work flows in the office, rather than merely asking customers what they need. That is, the focus is on identifying customer needs and then designing products to meet those needs.

■ What Is Your Personal Measure of Success?

As Table 5.1 indicates, the corporate measures of performance for Marketing and its affiliated groups do not always generate the appropriate incentives for optimizing value creation. Consequently it is particularly important for people in these areas to have personal measures of success that focus more broadly on value creation rather than just on the performance metrics for this function.

An illustration of this point is provided by a company that had a global expansion strategy calling for a significant presence in Asia. At the time the company was embarking on this strategy, its market share in Asia was negligible. The key was to quickly establish a clear brand awareness for its products in the region. To do so, significant resources had been earmarked the first year for advertising and other marketing initiatives.

Unfortunately, midway through the year, the company experienced a slowing down of its domestic (U.S.) business. The revised forecast was that earnings would fall short of both the company's projection and those of security analysts. The only apparent way to recover even part of the shortfall was to drastically cut expenses. Consequently, an across-the-board expense cut was ordered, including a dramatic reduction in the marketing budget for Asia.

Those involved in marketing in Asia complained bitterly about this decision. They viewed it as another example of corporate myopia, sacrificing the development of long-term brand equity in the interest of short-term earnings. To them it was just another illustration of the folly of worshiping at the altar of shareholder value!

It is hard to tell how much of the company's later difficulties in establishing a dominant and profitable position in Asia were due to this decision. The Asian crisis that followed resulted in a market meltdown for many companies. However, this case, more than a reflection of a right or wrong decision, points to the strikingly different ways in which those in Marketing and those in Senior Management or Finance sometimes view value creation.

To avoid falling into this trap, as a Marketing person you need to develop personal measures of success that are driven by what you believe are the key value drivers in the business. If you take a more comprehensive view of value creation that includes a strong Compete quadrant orientation, you will be better prepared to argue against value-destroying decisions that may be motivated solely by short-term financial pressures. You will also be able to allocate your resources better so that you preserve sufficient resources for the activities that create the most value.

■ Developing Speed

Speed in Marketing often has to do with shorter product development cycle times and faster reactions to changes in consumer preferences. It involves seizing first-mover advantages. Often it calls for rapid organizational transformation in anticipation of market trends. An excellent example is provided by Charles Schwab.

The First on the Street: Charles Schwab

San Francisco-based broker Charles Schwab first caught the attention of the investment world by introducing a business design innovation called "discount brokerage." Schwab went on to dominate this market for years. But then came the Internet, and the rules began to change. Brick-and-mortar financial service firms were put at a significant disadvantage as new providers began to offer cheaper on-line services.

Quietly Schwab began working behind the scenes to transform itself and transport the core of its business on-line. The reason for this profound transformation is that senior executives saw the enormous potential of the Internet before many others.[11] For instance, when the company noted in 1995 that PC sales in the United States outstripped television sales for the first time, it decided to commit significant resources to developing a viable on-line brokerage service.

Schwab also decided to make its on-line brokerage, Schwab.com, a separate business unit. This move was important to ensure that those who worked in Schwab.com were singularly focused on its success and not distracted by other responsibilities.

But not everything was smooth for Schwab. Whereas users of Schwab.com were charged $29.95 per trade, full-service customers of

Schwab were charged $65 to trade on-line. The two-tiered pricing policy was motivated by the worry that lowering trading charges for full-service customers trading on the Net would cannibalize the company's traditional brokerage business. Customers who were paying $65 per trade complained bitterly, however. Eventually, Schwab's co-CEO, David Pottruck, decided to stop worrying about cannibalization and jettisoned the two-tiered pricing, charging all customers $29.95 per on-line trade.

This decision resulted in lowering revenues by $150 million, and Schwab's stock price fell from $41 to $28. However, the setback was only temporary. By 1999 the company had 42 percent of all the assets invested in on-line-trading accounts in the United States, and Schwab.com was getting 76 million hits a day! Between mid-1998 and mid-1999, Schwab's stock price rose an astounding 329 percent.

The lessons from the Schwab case are clear:

- Recognize emerging trends and act on them before they become tidal waves.
- Never worry about cannibalization in a rapidly changing industry in which competitors move fast and are hard to identify.
- Always listen to the customer when a specific initiative is eliciting negative reactions.

None of these lessons are terribly profound, but it is amazing how many companies fail to heed them.

■ Organizational Success Strategies for Marketing and Affiliated Functions

Based on the content and case studies covered in this chapter, Figure 5.3 shows a model for success that can help move Marketing and its affiliated groups from their traditional Create quadrant position to one that permits a more well-rounded focus on value creation (refer to Figure 5.2).

What this figure summarizes is an expanded role for Marketing and its affiliated functions that takes them outside their traditional Create quadrant domain and builds a greater awareness of organization structure, market signals, and shareholder value.

It's interesting to relate the various activities in Figure 5.3 to the different quadrants of the Wholonics model. Since Marketing operates in both the Compete and Create quadrants, value-creation initiatives in this area must be judged accordingly. Existing products and routine product extensions must be managed in the Compete quadrant. The focus must therefore be on maximizing positive cash flow (maximizing sales, controlling expenses, and so on), controlling risk, and optimizing investment.

By contrast, many new product introductions must be managed in the Create quadrant. The rules change here. To generate substantial future value, both high risk and high investment may have to be tolerated. Moreover, positive cash flows in the short term may be very small or even nonexistent, as is exemplified by many Internet companies. Using Compete quadrant rules can end up suboptimizing value creation.

It is quite a challenge to accommodate the perspectives of the Compete and Create quadrants. One way to reconcile them is along the time dimension. Any significant breakthrough from the status quo—be it a product, a market, or a distribution channel innovation—begins in the Create quadrant. But if the innovation succeeds, it will be more fully developed and eventually will mature into the Compete quadrant.

■ Personal Success Strategies for Marketing and Affiliated Functions

At the personal level, there are four key points for people in Marketing and affiliated groups. First, the principles of success developed in the initial chapters of this book have powerful

What Does Value Mean? Identifying the Value Drivers	Develop Multiple Value-Creation Perspectives
• Develop a comprehensive definition of value and understand the entire value creation chain while making decisions such as how much SKU complexity to have, including the capital implications of these decisions • Focus your resources on the best product ideas. Don't spread yourself and the organization too thin.	• Develop a deep understanding between the short term and the long term in your organization, and communicate constantly in a cross-functional manner to make sure this understanding is shared across the organization. • Develop a deep understanding of the relevant financial tools and use them to evaluate things like product pricing and advertising expenditures. These tools are essential for ensuring that the Compete quadrant is not ignored. • Focus on controlling and managing risk and investments. • Position yourself more strongly in the Compete and Collaborate quadrants.

Figure 5.3. How Marketing and Affiliated Groups Can Optimize Value Creation

Develop Appropriate Strategy and Measures of Success	**Organize for Speed**
• Align your Marketing strategy with the overall corporate strategy and understand its implications for your Wholonics profile. • To generate new product ideas, don't do conventional market research. Figure out mechanisms for communicating with customers to understand their needs. Remember every unsolved customer problem is the best source of a new product idea. • Never let cannibalization stop you from introducing a new product with potential. Embrace risk. • Kill bad products with haste and don't stint on resources for good products. • Never hesitate to abandon even a successful product if you discover a better product to replace it.	• Organize the company by product, not geography. • Always search for innovations in sales and distribution channels and let these innovations drive your manufacturing processes. • If there is an intermediary between you and your customer, it is slowing down your ability to react to customer needs and you are not optimizing value creation. • Be prepared for profound organizational changes in anticipation of market trends.

applicability in these areas. Thus it is critically important to develop a personal success strategy that makes you stand out from others in your group.

Second, perhaps the easiest way to distinguish yourself is to develop an understanding of financial valuation principles and let these drive your pricing and product-introduction decisions. This is a traditional weakness of people in Marketing. If you can eliminate it and reflect your knowledge in the way you act, you will have a distinct advantage over others.

Third, you must master the two key activities of those in your group: defending existing products against competitive assaults and introducing new products. The former requires that you develop good Compete quadrant skills, and the latter requires that you develop good Create quadrant skills. Attending a course on creative thinking and innovation may help.

Finally, you should understand what you can personally do to develop multiple value-creation perspectives and improve your speed. As someone with a strong Create quadrant orientation, the "enemies" you need to get to know well are those in the opposite quadrant, which is Control. This means making friends with those in Manufacturing and Accounting. Also get to know the Finance folks who operate in the Control and Compete quadrants. Understand how they view value creation. What gets their motor running? You will become a much better value creator by understanding how they think.

CHAPTER SUMMARY

In this chapter I have discussed ways to use the five secrets of value creators to improve performance in Marketing, Sales and Distribution, and New Product Development. As defined in these areas, value tends to be within the narrow functional silo of Marketing, with some confusion about the distinction between value drivers and outcomes. This emphasizes the need to develop multiple value-creation perspectives that position Marketing more strongly in the Collaborate, Control, and Compete quadrants, reducing but not abandoning the traditional dominant Create quadrant positioning.

Marketing and its affiliated groups can have an important impact on strategy and move it more strongly in the direction of creating new products, even if these products significantly cannibalize the company's successful existing products. But Marketing also needs to become a significant force in the Collaborate quadrant. This will, of course, require closer collaboration with the Human Resources group, which is the topic of the next chapter.

Reflections and Discussion

Organizational Steps for Improving Value Creation in
Marketing, Sales and Distribution, and New Product Development

1. Conduct a survey of those in your Marketing and affiliated groups to construct the analog of Table 5.1 for your company. Summarize the lessons that you learn from this about how these functions view value creation and the effectiveness of the performance metrics being used for these functions. Develop an action plan to deal with these lessons.

2. Write down your Marketing and affiliated groups' strategy or strategies, each in three bullet points or less. Write a brief paragraph describing how each strategy is consistent with your overall corporate strategy. Be sure to (a) identify the key value drivers to which each strategy is linked and (b) specify the manner in which these strategies take a multiple-value-creation-perspectives approach that will position Marketing and its affiliated groups more in the Compete and Collaborate quadrants.

3. What distinguishes the strategies of your Marketing and affiliated groups from those of your competitors? How do these strategies create a sustainable competitive advantage for your organization?

4. What performance metrics do you have for measuring and rewarding speed in Marketing and its affiliated groups? How do you compare to your competitors on the dimension of speed?

5. How is your company organized? Take your senior executives (perhaps the top twenty-five) through an "envisioning exercise" in which they are asked to picture what the company would be like in five years in terms of decision making, new product introductions, and market positioning if it were organized completely along product or customer lines. If the new vision is attractive, examine the steps to transform the organization structure along those lines.

6. How many of your successful products have you cannibalized and replaced with even more successful products?

7. Benchmark your new product development process against the best-in-class companies discussed in this chapter. What are the lessons you can learn about how to improve your process?

Personal Steps for Improving Value Creation in
Marketing, Sales and Distribution, and New Product Development

1. Write down the ten most important activities you engage in and identify which quadrant each activity predominantly belongs to. Use your list to draw a Wholonics profile based on this. Then draw a *desired* Wholonics profile for yourself and identify at least three *new* activities you will have to engage in to help move you to the desired profile. Since the total amount of time available is the same as before, you will have to determine which of the ten activities you previously engaged in will be allocated less of your time now. Include in these activities at least one that involves getting to make new friends and the names of those from Accounting, Finance, and Manufacturing you will get to know better.

2. Write a brief personal statement of strategy that will produce actions on your part that will move you to your desired Wholonics profile. Make sure it is consistent with the three new activities identified in step 1. Also write a brief paragraph describing how your strategy will distinguish you from others in your organization, including an agenda for educating yourself about the tools of financial valuation.

3. Does your statement of strategy include ways to improve your creativity and innovativeness? If not, make sure you include a thoughtful approach to developing these skills.

4. Write down your personal measures of success, at least one of which differs from what your organization defines as performance assessment metrics for you. Ask yourself how your personal measures of success help you to overcome sunflower management.

5. Do you get tasks accomplished at a rate that surpasses others in your organization? Is your ability to do this improving through time? Develop an action plan to improve your speed, including parallel processing of multiple tasks.

Improving Value Creation in Human Resources

C oca-Cola has been one of the most spectacularly success- ful companies in the world in consistently creating out- standing shareholder value. In 1996, it was number one in terms of its aggregate value creation, with a Market Value Added (MVA)—the difference between its total market value and its book value—of almost $125 billion.

Most people who know Coke would argue that this success has been based on many factors—the outstanding brand equity of the product, Robert Goizueta's exceptional leadership, the adoption of Economic Value as a performance metric, and a very effective globalization campaign. Coca-Cola is not unique in having its success described in these terms—none of which, you'll notice, give any credit to HR management. Very rarely does one hear of HR management as a key driver of an organization's success in creating shareholder value.

Yet when companies encounter significant competitive challenges, HR leadership and management often become the focal points of constructive change to cope with these challenges. For example, some of Coca-Cola's problems in the late 1990s have been well publicized. Domestically it ran into an unusually aggressive campaign by PepsiCo for market-share leadership in the United States. It was also hurt by the economic slowdown in many countries where it had a significant presence. In Europe, it was hurt by product quality problems and the attendant negative publicity.

CEO Douglas Ivester, before announcing his retirement, undertook numerous initiatives to reshape the company to cope with these challenges more effectively. Perhaps his most important initiative was in the HR arena—changing the company's corporate culture.[1]

Despite its success, Coca-Cola has over the years come to be perceived as arrogant and bureaucratic. In its new environment, the company needed faster decision making and more empowered middle management. To address these issues, Ivester began shedding layers of the company's organizational hierarchy. The planning and budgeting processes were streamlined, and those in the field were given more decision authority. Employees were encouraged to be more creative and to take more risks.

In initiatives like these, Human Resources has a key role to play. If HR groups typically do not get nearly the respect commensurate with their potential for affecting value creation, it is largely because of the way they are perceived by the rest of the company. But HR groups themselves bear some of the responsibility. Too often they do not act like important strategic partners in the business. This lack of strategic partnership often stems from a lack of understanding of how true value creation pertains to HR.

Sometimes people disagree with me when I tell them that the potential value contribution of HR is underappreciated in the typical organization. My usual response is to ask them: "How often has someone from HR been made CEO in your company?" The answer: "Almost never."

It does not have to be this way. In the evolving world of e-commerce, HR groups can play a pivotal role in remaking organizations from within to learn how to play effectively by the new rules. But to do so HR personnel must reinvent themselves along the lines discussed in this chapter. In what follows, you will see how HR can make use of the five secrets of great value creators.

■ What Does Value Mean to You and Your Organization?

Developing an understanding of value is particularly important for HR because the output of the group tends to be intangible and often difficult to measure in hard dollars, while the cost of its services is very tangible and visible. Viewed this way, the impact of HR on organizational costs is more apparent than its impact on revenues. Consequently, whenever the organization is under pressure to perform financially, the HR budget becomes an attractive target for cuts. To combat this tendency the HR group needs to develop a strong understanding of value and communicate it effectively to the rest of the organization.

How should HR define its value contribution? One of the most important roles an HR group can play is to come up with innovations in organizational structure that can help employees behave in a manner that facilitates growth. HR also needs to develop a set of cultural diagnostic tools that help to monitor the pulse of the organization and determine when specific interventions are needed to keep the growth engine humming. Another key role is to lead education and training.

So an important value contribution of HR would be as a *growth facilitator.* Would this value be easy to measure? No. But it can be measured indirectly by looking at things like employee retention rates, the number of employees who truly believe their jobs are fun, the number of breakthrough product ideas coming to fruition, and so on.

To assess whether HR groups in various companies perceived their value in these terms, I surveyed HR professionals in a manner similar to those in the groups covered in earlier chapters. The findings are summarized in Table 6.1.

A number of interesting observations emerge from this evidence. First, although the performance metrics used in practice are collectively fairly comprehensive in their ability to assess the value contribution of HR, there is a strong focus on cost containment and transactional HR services. These are obviously important metrics, and performance in these dimensions is necessary for the smooth functioning of the organization. But when you look at how those in HR perceive value destruction and the manner in which the financial goals of the company impede value creation, you see that these metrics are paramount in terms of how much attention they command. In other words, while companies use a multitude of performance metrics for HR, the behavior of HR employees seems to be significantly influenced by goals related to cost containment, compliance, and limiting the risks associated with employee turnover, strikes, and related problems. These are all Control quadrant metrics. While such metrics drive behavior essential to the functioning of any hierarchy, a significant component of the value HR can add to the organization lies in the Collaborate quadrant.

Second, the performance metrics used in practice do include some from the Collaborate quadrant, for example, increasing employee retention and development of leadership and functional

Table 6.1. The Role of Human Resources in Value Creation

What performance metrics do you typically use?	How does your group create value? What are the value drivers you control?	How do you destroy value?	How do the financial goals of the company impede your value creation?	How would you like to redefine these goals?
■ Ability to manage vendors ■ Knowledge and ability to apply benefit policies ■ Talent assessment ■ Process management (HR transactions) ■ Project management (staffing) ■ Increasing employee retention ■ Departmental cost productivity ■ Employment status and union risk ■ Performance appraisals ■ Development of leadership and functional competencies ■ Relationship management development ■ Number of managers trained in HR compliance ■ Balanced scorecard	■ Helping to reduce the cost of running the business, including cost of reengineering and consolidating processes ■ Developing and placing the best talent ■ Improving talent retention ■ Changing compensation plan to link compensation to performance ■ Attracting talent ■ Reducing overall and departmental cost structure ■ Maintaining union-free status ■ Developing employee training programs that improve productivity	■ Ineffective interdepartmental communication ■ Too many meetings ■ Hiring the wrong people ■ Excessive focus on basic administrative and transactional work ■ Being involved in prolonged litigation with ex-employees to avoid setting precedent ■ Administration using inefficient systems ■ Excessive spending and inefficient use of resources	■ Diminished resources for staffing ■ Too many initiatives ■ Short-term financial focus that cuts back on resources for employee training ■ Excessive focus on cost structure and budgetary restrictions ■ Cutting back on the quality of the benefit package for employees	■ Use three or four simple goals and stick to them ■ Don't structure HR as a cost center ■ Give HR more of a profit and loss focus and responsibility ■ Take more of a long-term perspective on developing human resources ■ Create shareholder value while still making it personally worthwhile and valuable for employees to be with the organization

competencies. However, the important metric of leadership competency development is often not quantified in a way that allows it to become a powerful incentive. There is a relative paucity of organizations like PepsiCo in which the leadership development success of an individual is viewed as an important performance metric to determine whether that person should be promoted.

Third, as with other groups, there is a lack of clear understanding of the distinction between value drivers and desired outcomes. Things like attracting talent, improving talent retention, and reducing the cost of running the business are all desired outcomes, not value drivers. The value drivers that are likely to produce these desired outcomes are probably things like the organization's structure, its culture, the extent to which it encourages risk taking and empowerment, how enjoyable employees think their jobs are, and so on.

Fourth, the list of value-destroying activities is dominated by bureaucratic and procedural items. Those in HR seem to believe that a lot of the transactional work they do is not adding value. A likely reason is that this work absorbs far too much time to permit HR to develop a strategic partnership role with other parts of the organization and be an instrument of change. A key question for HR personnel, then, is how much of the transactional work can be outsourced.

Fifth, as in Manufacturing and Marketing and associated areas, HR employees are dismayed by the short-term financial pressures they face and view these as impeding value creation. This point is especially pertinent for HR, since the HR group's Collaborate quadrant initiatives are typically long-term in nature.

There is an intriguing suggestion that it would be useful to restructure HR as a profit center with Profit and Loss (P&L) responsibility. I believe that this is not a good idea for some staff support services, such as Finance, but the issue is not quite as obvious for HR.

One could think of an approach like the one AT&T used for Bell Labs, its research division. Since Bell Labs produces research, it was not organized with P&L responsibility. But then AT&T adopted Economic Value as a performance metric, and the decision was made to treat Bell Labs effectively as a P&L center. AT&T accomplished this in the following way. First, Bell Labs was given a budget for basic research, under the assumption that no AT&T unit would pay for *basic* research out of its own budget. Second, Bell Labs was asked to sell all of its *applied* research to other parts of AT&T. Since these other units were not obliged to buy this research if they did not perceive sufficient value relative to its price, AT&T effectively set up an *internal market* in which Bell Labs could sell its services. It would be interesting to consider a variant of this approach for at least some subset of HR activities.

Another interesting observation on this score is the apparent paradox in the responses that lack of cost containment is viewed as a way in which HR destroys value, but cost containment pressures imposed by the financial goals of the organization are also viewed as impeding HR's ability to create value. I will return to this point later.

Finally, Table 6.1 provides evidence of the four reasons why understanding of value gets blurred. There doesn't seem to be a single clear definition of value, and there is also a somewhat fuzzy recognition of value drivers. Excessive spending and inefficient use of resources are listed as value destroyers; these are examples of self-interested behavior that conflicts with value creation, as well as the negative zone of competition. The functional silo mentality seems evident in the way those in HR perceive their role in creating value. Other than the point about helping to reduce the cost of running the business, including reengineering and process-consolidation costs, most of the other activities listed under "How does your group create value?" are fairly traditional HR activities. Thus there is insufficient recognition of the cross-functional role HR can play in priming the organization's growth engine.

□

■ Multiple Value-Creation Perspectives

Traditionally HR has viewed itself as operating largely in the Collaborate and Control quadrants. This self-perception is evident in the performance metrics listed in Table 6.1. Activities such as developing organizational competencies belong in the Collaborate quadrant, whereas most of the transactional responsibilities of HR fall in the Control quadrant.

However, if HR is to be truly successful, it must learn how to develop an organization that is more effective in the Create quadrant. Many in HR seem to understand this point. But the mistake they commonly make is in believing that they simply need to do things in the background that enable others to be more innovative and to come up with great growth ideas. Those in HR themselves often don't understand the rules of the Create quadrant: how to be truly creative, how to make the whole organization more innovative and growth-driven. "Create" activities often end up being viewed as things that should be left to the CEO and other senior executives. Consequently, HR ends up failing to meet its true potential to contribute value to the organization.

Why does HR fall in this trap? I believe there are four reasons: HR's perception of itself as a staff support function, the belief of those in HR that they are HR specialists rather than experts in the business, the perception in other parts of the organization that HR is little more than an expense line in the company's budget, and the occasional view of those in HR that a "don't rock the boat" approach serves them best. Let's look at each of these factors.

HR as a Staff Support Function

The traditional perception by others of HR as a pure staff support function is often shared by HR professionals themselves. Since a staff support function is essentially a cost center, this perception creates a process orientation and bureaucratic mind-set. An unfortunate consequence is that the role that HR can play in facilitating the company's growth is often overlooked.

HR can facilitate growth through a variety of initiatives such as leadership development, design of appropriate performance metrics and incentive compensation schemes, development of training programs that teach employees to be effective and creative risk takers, realignment of the corporate culture so that it encourages employees to be empowered and explore bold initiatives, and creation of a constructive and open dialogue between different layers of the organization about change, growth, and effective communication. Unfortunately, the staff support mind-set of HR often stands in the way of the group's effectiveness in these growth-enhancing activities.

"We Are HR Specialists, Not Experts in the Business"

A second perception problem that stands in the way of HR's achieving its full potential in the organization is that the majority of the people in HR do not know as much about the business as they should. They are specialists in their own field, but often nowhere close to being at the level of line managers in their knowledge of the business the firm is involved in. This is to be expected. But taken to its extreme, it leaves HR personnel ill-equipped to participate meaningfully in value-creation initiatives, let alone lead them.

One way to address this problem is to rotate HR managers through other functions, including line responsibilities. This tactic has been employed to a limited extent in some companies. A second solution, which can complement the first, is training. The following case study illustrates this idea.

Back to (Business) School: Citibank

Citibank was not alone in its industry in recognizing that its HR managers were not bankers, they were HR specialists. Unlike many other banks, however, Citibank decided to do something about it. Around 1994, the bank decided to initiate a week-long training program in banking for its HR managers. The program was launched in 1995 on the University of Michigan campus prior to Citicorp's merger with Travellers. After the merger, the program was modified to include an insurance component to deal with that part of the combined entity's activities. The teaching is done by the university's business school faculty. I have been involved in this program since its inception.

The program is not designed to convert HR managers into Relationship managers or Product specialists for the bank—that's an unreasonable goal for any week-long program. And it is also unnecessary. After all, how much did Lou Gerstner know about information technology before being appointed CEO of IBM? Rather, the goal is to introduce participants to the basics of banking, the economics of the industry, recent trends, bank and capital market products, risk management strategies, operational issues, and the key leadership and management challenges HR managers need to confront in an organization like Citibank. In short, the objective is to make the HR managers more effective strategic partners in banking.

One of the interesting facts about Citibank is that in recent years it has hired a substantial number of people from outside the banking industry. The main reason is that the financial services industry has been undergoing a fundamental transformation and the pace of change is accelerating. Operating effectively in this environment calls for a variety of skills, many of which are quite different from the skills traditionally associated with bankers. Going outside the banking industry for talent has thus become an imperative.

As a consequence, many of the participants in the program at Michigan had been with the bank a very short time. Many had never worked in any bank before. The program therefore served three purposes. First, it provided a fairly thorough exposure to banking and new knowledge that could be used readily on the job. Second, it allowed the participants to learn about Citibank itself in a way that was normally not possible on the job because their day-to-day exposure was typically only to their operation within the bank. Third, it gave them an opportunity to get to know twenty-five or thirty of their colleagues. Relationships developed this way, on campus and away from work, are often long-lasting. They are particularly valuable to relatively new employees who have not yet had a chance to get to know others in the organization.

At the end of one of these programs, one of the participants summed up the value of the program to her as follows:

> I think I now understand where all the pieces fit together in the bank. I believe I can now participate meaningfully in business discussions with the line managers I support and help make better decisions within our group. The language of banking will no longer be a barrier between me and those who serve external clients or design products.

Others' Perception of HR as a Line in the Expense Budget

I have had numerous conversations with line managers in organizations who view their HR colleagues as providers of basic transactional services such as dealing with the union, handling compliance issues, and taking care of employee severance packages. Everything else done by HR—including leadership development and executive training—was considered by many as adding to the expense budget rather than to value creation and hence as quite dispensable.

Such a perception can be a big roadblock for an HR group that is seeking to develop people within the organization. Here is a classic illustration that I have seen play out in company after company: HR participates in developing and scheduling an executive education program, and then it can't get senior executives to release their people to participate, especially when their part of the business is not doing well. Developing capabilities in people, it seems, often competes with managing the business.

This, of course, is not surprising. In fact, it is the natural order of things. Managing a business on a day-to-day basis calls for mostly Control and Compete quadrant competencies. Developing capabilities in people deals with competencies that reside in the Collaborate quadrant. As noted earlier, the Collaborate and Compete quadrants are often in conflict.

Ironically the people in the HR group itself often unwittingly contribute to this perception. Whenever there is pressure on them to limit their budgets, they begin to judge their leadership and competency development initiatives on the basis of cost rather than value added to the organization. Indeed, in the absence of a deep and shared understanding of how HR creates value, it's all too easy to focus primarily on what is easy to measure—cost—and avoid the harder task of measuring value in meaningful ways. And if HR assesses its own contribution primarily on a cost basis, why is it surprising that others in the organization tend to think of it as little more than an expense line?

To escape this trap, HR personnel must first change how they think about their value contribution and what they focus on. Their emphasis must shift from cost containment to organizational growth. And they must find ways to communicate to others the tangible ways in which they are helping the organization grow.

Don't Rock the Boat: The "Nothing Beats the Status Quo" Mind-set

The simple fact of the matter is this: A lot of people preach change, but nobody really likes it. Some embrace change more readily than others, but typically you have to give people *incentives* to change. HR can play a central role in designing the appropriate incentives and organizational culture for radical, value-enhancing change.

Unfortunately, the last thing that some HR groups want is radical change in the organization. Maintaining the status quo means they can focus on the transactional HR services of the Control quadrant—such as figuring out clever ways to cut costs and stay within the budget without offending too many people. There is low risk in this course of action, less of a chance of angering others in the organization. "Peace and pay" is what it's called.

Being an agent of change, by contrast, is inherently risky for anyone. No matter how well you understand the company's strategic direction, there is always a chance that your change efforts will produce the wrong results. Good people may leave. Those who stay may exhibit more self-interested behavior than before at the expense of the organization. You could be fired or made irrelevant. And the less you truly understand the business your organization is in—the less of a strategic business partner you are—the more risky change will appear to you. In other words, you are more likely to maintain the status quo the vaguer you are about what value means to you and your organization and how *you* can help the organization grow.

In the most successful organizations, however, change is an almost constant phenomenon. What people in HR can do is to lead change. They can do this in many ways. One way to is to sponsor skills development initiatives for employees at various levels in the organization. Another is to help identify and develop into organizational leaders people with an open mind, passion, and a willingness to embrace change.

A third way to rock the boat and change the status quo is to be at the vanguard of initiatives to implement new incentive compensation systems that encourage employees to think outside the box, stretch themselves, and bring an ownership mind-set to their work. Indeed, the most powerful tool an HR person can use to help the organization grow is to come up with effective ways to make employees feel and behave like owners.

In summary, HR groups that fail to realize their full potential as value creators tend to have Wholonics profiles that are heavily skewed in favor of Control quadrant activities. As Figure 6.1 shows, they need to be positioned more strongly in the other quadrants.

In particular, HR needs to become more effective in the Collaborate and Create quadrants. In the Collaborate quadrant, HR needs to improve its effectiveness in building high-performance, empowered teams on which individuals have a strong ownership mind-set. In the Create quadrant, effort has to be devoted to elevating the creative abilities of those in HR, as well as their understanding of the business. Smaller improvements must be

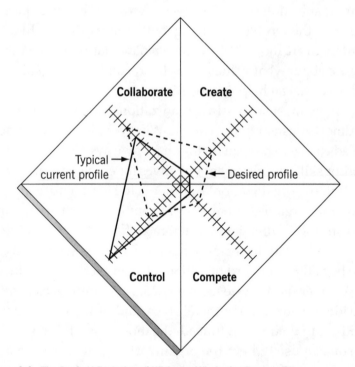

Figure 6.1. The Desired Evolution of HR in the Wholonics Perspective

made in the Compete quadrant in terms of becoming more effective in competing for human talent in the labor market. These activities are enormously important, but they will probably need less emphasis in the Wholonics effort as they are already being performed quite well by good HR groups.

Figure 6.1 is not meant to suggest that the transactional activities of HR in the Control quadrant are unimportant. Rather, it suggests that the organizational resources devoted to these activities could perhaps be conserved by outsourcing in order to free up resources for activities in the Collaborate and Create quadrants.

■ What Is Your Business Strategy?

Developing a deep understanding of corporate strategy is critical for HR for two reasons. First, HR can play a vital role in helping to devise an effective way to communicate the strategy to everybody in the organization. Second, a deep knowledge of strategy is essential for coming up with ways to improve creativity and foster growth.

But a mere understanding of strategy is not enough; HR must also be proactive in shaping strategy. As part of the team that devises strategy, HR personnel can bring to the table their knowledge of the people in the organization and thereby help improve the team's understanding of what is strategically possible, determine changes in the organizational culture that are necessary to make the strategy more successful, and energize the organization around the strategy. All of this requires HR to be involved in the formulation and implementation of strategy. Although this happens relatively infrequently, the following case study shows that the best-in-class recognize the importance of linking strategy to the management of human resources.

HR Strategy Among the Giants: Microsoft

With a market capitalization of over $600 billion, Microsoft was the world's most valuable company until recently surpassed by Cisco. It would be very easy for such a successful company to bask in its past success and be satisfied with the status quo.

But not Microsoft. After being named president of Microsoft, Steven A. Ballmer—now CEO—conducted numerous in-depth interviews with employees in 1998 and 1999 and concluded that the company had become too bureaucratic and complex to compete effectively with its swifter Internet rivals. In Ballmer's words: "We needed to give people a beacon that they could follow when they are having a tough time with prioritization, leadership, where to go, what hills to take."[2]

As a result, Microsoft has launched "Vision Version 2," a major overhaul of the strategic thinking and structure at the company. The company's previous vision statement ("a PC on every desk and in every home") was replaced with "giving people the power to do anything they want, anywhere they want, and on any device." With this shift, Microsoft programmers became free to develop products that did not revolve around Windows software.

The overhaul was necessitated by the new breed of Internet companies with which Microsoft must compete. Ten thousand new Web sites appear every day, and companies are creating new products and offering them to customers at breakneck speed. Compared to these companies, Microsoft looks bureaucratic, if for no other reason than its sheer size. With thirty thousand employees, almost two hundred different products, and at least five layers of management, Microsoft can't make decisions nearly as fast as it used to. One consequence has been a disturbing departure of talent. High-potential employees have left either to start up Internet companies or to join existing Internet players.

Under Vision Version 2, the company is to be reorganized into eight new groups that would be more attuned to the needs of customers rather than the company's technology wizards. Levels below the key executives were given more decision-making autonomy. As Ballmer said: "I have to grow from being a leader to being a leader of leaders."[3]

What is interesting about this case study is that Microsoft, a technology company, did not view its challenge for the future as technological. Rather, it viewed the challenge as one of managing its human resources. The Microsoft case illustrates two important points for HR:

1. There is no better time to change corporate culture than when the company is doing well. When a company is under financial stress, it is often too late to think about cultural change, a Collaborate quadrant activity. The focus, by necessity, has to be almost exclusively on Compete quadrant initiatives, which are typically opposed to what is needed in the Collaborate quadrant.
2. The best way for HR to learn whether the organization needs change and what type of change may be needed is to talk to employees. In addition, HR should study the needs of the company's customers and examine the speed and effectiveness with which emerging (often latent) competitors are changing the rules of the game.

■ What Is Your Personal Measure of Success?

The excessive focus on the Control quadrant in terms of the performance metrics that dominate the behavior of HR managers is apparent from Table 6.1. One implication is that people in HR need to develop their own personal measures of success that allow them to create value rather than get caught up in the usual transactional orientation of others in the group.

Another danger for HR personnel to guard against is sunflower management. This problem tends to be more severe in HR than in any other functional area because sunflower management increases in severity as performance becomes harder to assess objectively. So one way to combat sunflower management is to link employee compensation to hard, objective measures of performance. Doing so creates a stronger incentive for employees to do what is right rather than what they think their superiors want to see. Unfortunately, when objective measures of performance are unavailable, you have to rely on subjective performance measures. These measures are usually far less effective in producing incentives to avoid sunflower management, since the assessment of performance now depends on the boss's subjective judgment. As a result, employees are tempted to act in a manner that they believe will positively influence that subjective judgment.

This problem is severe for HR because many of its activities lack hard, objective measures of performance. Still, there are numerous examples of individuals who have resolved these problems effectively. One example is provided by the case study discussed next.

Training for Results: Whirlpool Corporation

In 1993, Whirlpool Corporation, the world's largest appliance manufacturer, decided to launch an ambitious training program for a few hundred of its financial analysts. The training was designed to acquaint analysts with cutting-edge resource allocation tools they were likely to need for assessing major capital investment proposals. As then-CFO Michael Callahan said, "Over the next five years, we will be making over $2 billion in capital investments. This is like going to war. If my financial analysts are like fighter pilots, I want them to be well trained in how to fly those planes. I want them to be sure of themselves when they make investment recommendations."

I was part of a faculty team that was asked to develop this program. What is interesting is that we were chosen for the task by a *cross-functional* team of upper middle managers who were assigned the responsibility of selecting the group to develop and deliver the program and also to work with the group during the design phase. The Whirlpool cross-functional team included one HR representative.

The basic premise of the program was that it would be *performance-based.* In other words, we were going to develop only those tools and skills that the participants would need to perform up to expectations on the job. Anything that was "nice to know" but not needed for on-the-job performance was to be excluded. Moreover, to simulate the actual work environment, the program had to focus on both individual training and group work. There was also a great deal of emphasis on training participants to be independent in their thinking and to do what was in the shareholders' best interests, not what they perceived senior management wanted.

To design such a program, we needed to know the following:

- What should the new resource allocation system look like for it to be world-class and be aligned with the company's strategy?
- What skills and knowledge would financial analysts need to perform well in such a system? What kind of mind-set did they need to stand by the results of their analysis?
- What were the current levels of skills and knowledge in the organization and hence the gaps that needed to be filled to get to the desired level of performance?
- What is the optimal design of a program to deliver these skills and knowledge?

Step 1 required benchmarking various companies that were reputed to have world-class resource allocation systems. Once this task was completed, our group met with the Whirlpool team to arrange extensive interviews with various company groups from different parts of the world in Manufacturing and Technology, Marketing, Sales and Distribution, Finance, and so on. The purpose of the interviews was to gain insights into the problems people perceived with the existing system that the new system would attempt to overcome and to understand the current level of skills and knowledge in the organization. We then designed a new resource allocation system that was customized to the strategic needs of the company. This proposal was presented to the CFO and his direct reports for feedback and approval.

The next step was for our group to meet with the Whirlpool team to prepare a description of the skills and knowledge that would be needed to perform effectively in the new system. With this assessment completed, we had a list of the gaps between the skills and knowledge that were needed and those that existed in the company. This gap analysis then formed the starting point for designing the program.

The program design was greatly facilitated by the presence of the cross-functional Whirlpool team. This was a team of unusually highly motivated people. We spent an intensive week together to get started. The workday typically began at 7 A.M. and ended around 10 P.M. One day we were having dinner when a colleague of one of our team members happened to be passing by. Observing how late we were working, he asked this team member, "How much of your annual performance is going to depend on this project? I hope it's a lot, given how much time you're spending on this." Our team member replied, "Zero. But it doesn't matter. This is important for the company. Besides, Mike Callahan knows I am doing this."

The final step was to take the senior Finance executives of the company—CFO Mike Callahan and his direct reports—through an abbreviated version of the program. Our objective was threefold. First, this was the group that the target audience reported to, either directly or through another level in the organization, so having these executives aware of the kind of financial analysis that the participants would produce after completing the program was essential for completing the loop. That is, we wanted to make sure that there was on-the-job reinforcement of the skills developed in the program, with senior management conditioned to expect and demand the quality of output commensurate with the training. Second, we wanted feedback from the senior Finance group to change the program design if necessary. Third, there were some important open questions about the design of the resource allocation system itself that we wanted resolved.

As is the case in most large companies, it was not easy to get a group like this together for two to three days for this purpose, but we felt very strongly that doing so was essential to the overall success of the program. Because the CFO was strongly committed to the initiative and the HR group played a constructive role in the process, the meeting with the senior Finance group was arranged.

The two-and-a-half-day meeting turned out to be enormously valuable in meeting all three of our goals. There was a sense of great excitement as we began our delivery of the training program a few weeks later. By the end of the year (1994), almost two hundred participants had been through the program.

This case illustrates some valuable points for HR managers in any business:

- Every good executive education and development program is an organizational change initiative in disguise. Thus an explicit objective should be to change behavior in tangible ways, and there should be an identification of the kind of behavior desired as a result of the program (the change initiative). Don't be surprised when a good executive education program starts a corporate revolution.
- To effect change, it is best to link the education to the performance that is expected of participants on the job. Start with the assumption that executive education should be performance-based—and choose a different approach only if this assumption is proven to be inappropriate in the context of the situation.
- There should be an internal, cross-functional team that is involved in helping to design any executive education program or change initiative.
- Like our team members who gave unstintingly of their time despite the lack of an explicit reward for doing so, you need a personal measure of success that exceeds organizational expectations.
- Executive education can be an effective tool to combat sunflower management because it can make employees more sure of themselves and emphasize to them the enormously positive value-creation implications of standing by the truth.

- Any executive education program must involve senior management as well. If this is not done, senior management will not consistently demand of the participants the performance that the program is designed to deliver; their expectations may still be governed by what they were conditioned to accept prior to the program. The desired organizational change may then fail to materialize. Remember a simple rule: if the program isn't worth the time of senior management, it probably isn't worth the time of the participants!

■ Developing Speed

People rarely associate speed with the HR group. After all, building communities and competencies within the organization takes time. Nevertheless, there is no reason why HR cannot participate in helping design the organization's structure and information communication systems to speed up decision making. A good example is provided by Cisco.

Networking Reach: Cisco Systems

Based in San Jose, California, Cisco Systems is the global leader in networking for the Internet. Its annual revenues in 1998 were over $8 billion, and its market capitalization was about $100 billion. By early 2000, Cisco had a market capitalization of over half a trillion dollars, and had surpassed Microsoft as the most valuable company in the world.

What is perhaps most impressive about Cisco is its corporate culture and its organization design. Its CEO, John T. Chambers, described Cisco as follows:

- Built on change, not stability;
- Organized around networks, not a rigid hierarchy;
- Based on interdependencies of partners, not self-sufficiency; and
- Constructed on technological advantage, not bricks and mortar.[4]

The key to Cisco's organizational design is its networks. Because Cisco itself builds the powerful networks that link businesses to their customers and suppliers, it has found it convenient to use that technology to transform its own organization.

The network seamlessly links the various stakeholders of the company—its customers, business partners, suppliers, and employees. Cisco does over $5 billion of business over the Internet, and 70 percent of customer requests for technical support are filled electronically. Customer satisfaction rates are higher than those possible with human interaction, because the variability in the quality of support that is unavoidable with human interaction is absent here and also because customers who make these requests do not need to speak to a live person. Moreover, the approach economizes on the number of engineers needed for technical support. These engineers can be used for new product development, which gives Cisco a significant competitive advantage.

The network is also the engine that makes the company work from within. It connects Cisco with its suppliers, contract manufacturers (the company outsources 70 percent of its production), and assemblers, making the entire group look like a single company to the outsider. For example, outside contractors use the company's intranet to learn about orders from Cisco's customers and then ship the product directly to the customer the same day—in a box that Cisco never touches!

Cisco also uses the network to recruit talent. More than half of all the job applications it receives are filed electronically. Moreover, employees are able to use the Net to access information ranging from company event schedules to expense report status.

Despite this extensive use of technology, Cisco has not abandoned human interaction and the personal touch. Chambers schedules quarterly meetings with employees, invites all employees in the month of their birth to hour-and-a-half "birthday breakfasts," and strives constantly to encourage open and direct communication between employees and all of Cisco's leaders.

Cisco puts so much emphasis on corporate culture that it never acquires a company whose values and culture are very different from its own. On issues of compensation, the Cisco culture emphasizes ownership more than wages. About 40 percent of the stock options at the company are held by individual (non-executive) employees.

Cisco is also remarkably nonhierarchical for a company of its size. Chambers says, "You never ask your team to do something you wouldn't do yourself." As proof of this, Chambers flies coach like all other employees. And perhaps just as impressively, there are no reserved parking spaces for senior executives at Cisco headquarters.

The Cisco case study emphasizes the following points:

- Using the full potential of electronic networks allows a company to minimize the physical and human assets it owns. Networks can create links between customers, suppliers, business partners, and employees. This provides speed in executing initiatives, a flattening of the corporate hierarchy, and the creation of a fast-moving, action-oriented corporate culture.
- Use stock option plans—not limited to top management— to make employees into owners.
- Never ignore the personal touch. Emphasize to your leaders that they should spend as much face time as possible with employees—coaching, mentoring, and having dialogues about strategy, customers, and organizational issues.
- Get rid of corporate status symbols. That includes distinctions between employees by rank in terms of class of air travel, special executive dining rooms, and reserved parking spaces. If you are part of the HR group in your company and the company has any of these practices, make it your priority to try and eliminate them.

■ Organizational Success Strategies for Human Resources

Numerous organizations have successfully managed their human resources in a way that elevates human capital to a position of central importance in value creation. One such organization is Tricon.

Culture on the Menu: Tricon

Tricon, which owns Kentucky Fried Chicken, Taco Bell, and Pizza Hut, states six goals that govern its strategy and decisions. The very first goal is to "become renowned for an ownership and recognition culture that drives the best results in the industry." A prominent page in Tricon's 1998 Annual Report displays the company's message in bold letters (captured in Figure 6.2).

Tricon emphasizes celebrating the achievements of its employees, and it makes a special point of noting that it has fun doing it. Pride in one's work and a passion for excellence are repeatedly emphasized as corporate mottoes.

Too often, companies say the same things that Tricon says, but in ways that are meaningless to employees. What Tricon seems to have figured out is that long, flowery prose that extols "the virtues of employee commitment and hard work and the central importance of customer satisfaction" often leaves employees cold. Such prose has a lot of fancy words that would make a high school English teacher proud. But it is entirely ineffectual as a communication device to make employees internalize the message. Tricon offers an example of how to do it right. What lessons can be drawn from this example?

First, translate the message into a simple language that is closely related to the business you are in, so that employees can connect with it. Here is how Tricon explains its people capability focus in its 1998 Annual Report:

We know that when we recognize and reward great behavior, we'll have a charged-up, customer focused team. So we've come

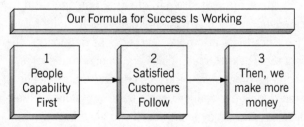

Figure 6.2. **The Tricon Motto**

up with some rather unusual awards to recognize leadership: Bulldogs and Floppy Chickens at KFC, Big Cheese Awards at Pizza Hut, the Royal Order of the Pepper at Taco Bell, the Globe at TRI and a special YUM Award at Tricon. Winning these awards is a big deal in our company, because those who do are committed to quality food and satisfying our customers better than anyone.[5]

There are many companies that have awards for outstanding perform-ance. But how many of them give these awards such entertaining names and highlight the awards as well as the winners in their Annual Reports?

Second, emphasize *visual* communication of important messages. The Tricon Annual Report is filled with interesting pictures and other strik-ing visual images of the company's products, people, awards, and guid-ing principles. Even a casual and brief look at the annual report can leave a person with a lasting impression of the most important messages the company wants to convey:

- Our employees come first; they are capable and they have fun doing their jobs.
- Motivated employees and good products lead to high customer sat-isfaction.
- With satisfied customers, we do well for our shareholders.

One of the biggest weaknesses in HR groups in major corporations is that these groups do not communicate very effectively with other parts of the organization. A big reason for this ineffectiveness is the insufficient use they make of visual communication.

Finally, have fun and strive to create an organization culture and workplace environment in which all employees have fun. It is a curious medical fact that there are more heart attacks on Monday than on any other day of the week! Human beings are unique in this regard in the an-imal kingdom; no other creature knows one day of the week from another. The only reasonable explanation seems to be work-related stress and that a lot of people do not enjoy their jobs. If you need further proof, just tune in to any radio station on late Friday afternoon to listen to the rejoicing over the end of the work week, and then tune in on Monday to listen to the moaning. Creating a fun work environment should be one of the major objectives of any HR group.

Has all this paid off for Tricon? Financial performance in 1998 was quite impressive. Store-level profit margins grew to 13.5 percent, excluding unusual charges and net gains from facility actions. Operating profits increased 11 percent in 1998—and would have been 43 percent except for the negative impact of foreign currency translation. Earnings per share grew a healthy 29 percent.

Using the Tricon case study as well as the earlier discussions, Figure 6.3 presents a model of how HR can maximize value creation.

Figure 6.3 provides insights about HR's role. Since HR must operate in all quadrants, with a focus on developing new capabilities in the Collaborate and Create quadrants, it faces the formidable challenge of developing an appreciation of conflicting viewpoints. When it is operating in the Control quadrant, its objective is to minimize (hopefully eliminate) risk. Such Control quadrant activities include minimizing labor risk by helping the organization avoid litigation, strikes, unexpected turnover, and the like. Moreover, in the Control quadrant, HR also attempts to increase positive cash flow by reducing expenses and staying within budget.

But HR must acknowledge a different set of rules in the Collaborate and Create quadrants. On the issue of risk, HR must help develop organizational capabilities that equip the organization to react rapidly to changes in the competitive structure of the industry. Unlike its role in the Control quadrant, this requires actually fostering a risk-seeking culture in which employees are empowered to take risks, be creative, and have fun. Similarly, on the issue of cash flow, the goal should not be to just reduce the cost structure. On the contrary, investments in training and the

What Does Value Mean? Identifying the Value Drivers	Develop Multiple Value-Creation Perspectives
• Have a clear definition of how you add value and the underlying drivers that affect your ability to create value. • Focus on facilitating organizational growth as a motivating goal. To do this effectively, learn the business you are in and how competitors and latent competitors are organizing and competing with you. • Use cost efficiency as a value measure for transactional services but not for growth enhancement activities. • Work on how others in the organization perceive you. Is your value contribution clear to everyone?	• Develop the mind-set that HR is an instrument of organizational change and growth, not merely a staff support function. • Become sufficiently knowledgeable about the business to be an effective strategic partner with line managers. • Change the perception of others that you are a little more than a line in the expense budget by changing the focus of your activities from the transactional services of the Control quadrant to activities in the Collaborate and Create quadrants. Outsource as many transactional services as possible. • The status quo is usually not something you should consider acceptable.

Figure 6.3. How HR Can Maximize Value Creation

Develop Appropriate Strategy and Measures of Success	Organize for Speed
• Develop personal measures of success around facilitating organizational growth and creating an ownership mind-set in employees that exceeds organizational expectations. • Devise appropriate incentive compensation plans and use them on a broad-based basis to help create an ownership mind-set. • Develop an understanding of your organization's strategy and participate in its formulation and implementation. • Remember that the best time to change the organization is when it is doing well. • Avoid limiting your view of training to its immediate goals—every employee training program is a change agenda in disguise besides being a tool to develop capabilities in your people. • Use training as an effective tool to combat sunflower management. • Use passion, conviction, and enthusiasm to constantly communicate in visual ways to your employees how they can create value. • Create an environment in which employees have fun.	• Use networks to flatten the corporate hierarchy, improve execution speed, and link employees, customers, suppliers, and business partners. • Get rid of corporate status symbols to create a greater spirit of community and affection among employees.

development of organizational capabilities should be made even though they will reduce positive cash flow totals in the short run.

This observation helps resolve the apparent paradox in Table 6.1, where the data show that both excessive spending and cost containment are viewed negatively by HR. Cost containment is critically important in the Control quadrant, so that exceeding budget on transactional HR services related to HR projects and processes is a value destroyer. However, constraints on resources to develop organizational capabilities and culture through training and other initiatives that belong to the Collaborate and Create quadrants also destroy value. One of the biggest challenges for HR leadership is to balance these competing forces.

■ Personal Success Strategies for Human Resources

There are obvious implications for anyone in HR in Figure 6.3, as far as formulating a personal success strategy is concerned. I will recap these shortly. But first I want to discuss a case study that illustrates how personal leadership in HR can be a powerful instrument of constructive organizational change.

HR Leads the Way to Survival: Federal-Mogul Corporation

Federal-Mogul Corporation is a $2 billion auto parts manufacturer and distributor based in Detroit.[6] Beginning in 1990, the company built an extensive chain of retail outlets throughout Europe, Latin America, Africa, and Australia. However, in the process it strayed away from its core business—making automobile parts and components for original equipment manufacturers. Eventually, this strategy caused Federal-Mogul's stock price to decline from about $40 per share in 1993 to just $16 by the third quarter of 1996.

The drop in stock price led to the replacement of the CEO by an insider, Steve Miller, who then recruited Richard Snell from Tenneco Automotive to replace him. Snell took over as CEO in November 1996, and appointed Thomas Ryan as his CFO. Snell and Ryan decided to adopt Economic Value—which they referred to as EVA—for performance measurement and compensation in 1997. The implementation of EVA was planned to take place between June 1997 and April 1998.

An important part of the implementation was to install EVA as a mind-set, and this involved training and communication. The task was entrusted to Dick Randazzo, the head of HR. It was Randazzo's job to convince the organization that EVA was not principally a finance initiative. *Rather, it was intended to change behavior.*

Randazzo and his team were also instrumental in dispelling the misperception that the new measure would be used to rank and dismiss managers. They explained to managers that what mattered was the improvement in EVA, and not where one started.

Finally, Dick Randazzo and his team also made numerous business recommendations, such as how to calculate EVA profit and why it was useful to consolidate EVA significantly above the level of plants and geographic regions.

In short, the head of HR in this case led a cross-functional team that spearheaded the effort to remake the organization. EVA was a convenient instrument of that charge, but it took the people within Federal-Mogul to make it all happen.

The financial results were spectacular. By September 1997, the company's stock price had risen to $45. Encouraged by the initial success of this change initiative, Snell redefined the company's sales target as $10 billion by 2002, a quintupling of revenue from 1996!

Based on this case study and the earlier discussions, I can now summarize how you can develop your own personal success strategy in HR.

First, stop thinking like a staff support person. Learn the business. Take management development programs in Marketing, Finance, and Manufacturing. Learn how your company makes its products, how it markets them, how it analyzes investment decisions financially, how it generates new product ideas. Ask for a job rotation that requires you to assume line responsibilities.

Second, develop a deep understanding of your company's strategy. Figure out the best way to communicate the strategy to others. Develop an action plan that permits you to participate in its active implementation and in helping your company grow.

Third, think of creative ways to instill in employees an ownership mind-set. As the Federal-Mogul case indicates, one of the easiest ways to encourage this mind-set is by adopting an effective incentive compensation program. You should play a leadership role in attempting to uncover the kinds of behavior that your current incentive compensation program produces in employees, and to decide whether this is the kind of behavior you want for optimizing value creation. If not, how can you change the current program for the better?

Fourth, cultivate deep personal relationships with key external partners who can help you in designing initiatives to develop the necessary capabilities in the managerial and executive talent in your organization. Remember that developing talent is a Collaborate quadrant activity, not a Control quadrant activity. That means your focus should be on how effectively the necessary capabilities are being developed—not on the cost of developing them. Moreover, your goal should be to make your external partners feel like partners, not vendors. Try to develop in them the same kind of ownership mind-set you are seeking to instill in your fellow employees. True partnership will facilitate this. But remember that true partnership means collaborating in coming up with solutions that maximize value creation. It is not haggling over price or keeping information from each other to gain the upper hand in negotiations.

Finally, make it your mission to help the organization constantly change and evolve. Take the lead in identifying ways to make your current organization obsolete and to develop an organizational culture in which people embrace such change.

CHAPTER SUMMARY

This chapter went into detail on how HR personnel can use the five secrets of value creators. The meaning of value can sometimes get blurred for HR because of a strong focus on cost containment and transactional services. Although these Control quadrant activities are important, they distract HR from its core mission of creating the appropriate organization culture, a Collaborate quadrant activity. Moreover, HR can play a powerful role in priming the organization's growth pump.

Doing this effectively requires the appropriate multiple perspectives on value creation. Standing in the way are four impediments: (1) HR's perception of itself as a staff support function, (2) the belief by those in HR that they are HR specialists rather than experts in the business, (3) the perception in other parts of the organization that HR is little more than an expense line in the company's budget, and (4) the occasional view of those in HR that the status quo is best. This chapter covered practical ways to overcome these impediments and position HR more strongly in the Collaborate and Create quadrants.

It also discussed how HR can become more proactive in shaping strategy. The Microsoft case study illustrates how much importance leading companies attach to the management of their human resources in realigning the company's strategic direction.

On the issue of personal measures of success, the chapter focused on employee training and executive education as mechanisms to combat sunflower management. As the Whirlpool case study illustrates, every good executive education initiative should be part of an organizational change agenda.

Finally, although speed is not typically associated with HR, the Cisco case study illustrated how a company can organize its people and decision-making processes to improve its speed. HR should be leading such organizational attempts to improve speed.

Reflections and Discussion

Organizational Steps for Improving
Value Creation in Human Resources

1. Conduct a survey of those in your HR group to construct the analog of Table 6.1 for your company. Summarize the lessons that you learn about how this function views value creation and the effectiveness of

the performance metrics being used for it. Develop an action plan to deal with these lessons.

2. Write down your HR strategy in three bullet points or less. Write a brief paragraph describing how the strategy is consistent with your overall corporate strategy. Be sure to (a) identify the key value drivers to which the strategy is linked and (b) specify the manner in which the strategy takes a multiple-value-creation-perspectives approach that will position HR more in the Collaborate and Create quadrants.

3. What distinguishes your HR strategy from those of your competitors? How does your strategy create a sustainable competitive advantage for your organization?

4. What has your HR group done to improve the speed of decision making in your organization? How do you compare to your competitors on the dimension of speed?

5. What specific things does HR do to help your organization grow? What new activities does it need to engage in to facilitate growth?

6. Do a survey to determine the kinds of behavior your current compensation structure is producing. Pay particular attention to the perverse behaviors it produces. How would you modify your compensation structure to minimize such behavior?

7. What management development programs has HR been associated with in your company in the last five years that have resulted in dramatic and positive change in how the company works? Develop an action plan to launch at least one such program every two years.

8. Conduct an analysis of the time spent by HR in providing transactional services versus developing organizational capabilities. Have you performed a cost-benefit analysis on outsourcing these transactional services?

9. How much fun do employees think it is to work in your company? Do you have a quantifiable way of judging how effectively your HR group is developing the appropriate organizational culture?

Personal Steps for Improving Value Creation in Human Resources

1. Write down the ten most important activities you engage in and identify which quadrant each activity predominantly belongs to. Use your list to draw a Wholonics profile. Then draw a *desired* Wholonics profile for yourself and identify at least three *new* activities you will have to

engage in to help move you to the desired profile. Since the total amount of time available is the same as before, you will have to determine which of the ten activities you previously engaged in will be allocated less of your time now. Include in these activities at least one that involves making new friends. List the names of people from Manufacturing, Finance, and Marketing, Sales, and New Product Development that you will get to know better.

2. Write a brief personal statement of strategy that will produce actions on your part that will move you to your desired Wholonics profile and that is consistent with the three new activities identified in step 1. Also write a brief paragraph describing how your strategy will distinguish you from others in your organization.

3. Write down your personal measures of success, at least one of which differs from what your organization defines as performance assessment metrics for you. Ask yourself how your personal measures of success help you to overcome sunflower management.

4. How much of your time do you personally spend on transactional activities versus personal development and activities that help the organization grow? Develop an action plan to drop at least 50 percent of your transactional activities and to use this time to (a) learn the business better, (b) acquire personal capabilities in areas like Marketing and Finance, (c) develop initiatives that create more of an ownership mind-set in employees. Write a plan for forming personal relationships with external partners who can help you develop initiatives to improve the capabilities of managers and leaders in your organization.

7

Improving Value Creation in Finance

t is by design that the Finance group is the last one to be dealt with in this book. Of all the areas in an organization, none has greater responsibility for making sure that the organization is constantly focused on value creation.

The role of Finance in ensuring the financial health and continuity of an organization cannot be overemphasized. There are endless examples of outstanding companies that have found themselves on the hot seat because they did not deliver sufficient shareholder value. Although Nike may well be the second most well-known brand in the world (after Coke), the company was sailing in rough waters in mid-1998. Talks of layoffs and other cuts were rampant. Why? Excess inventory in the United States and Asia and subpar performance on other shareholder-value dimensions.

And then there is Kodak. Among the many challenges former CEO George Fisher faced early in his tenure, perhaps his most pressing was to dramatically improve the company's cost structure and improve its capital productivity. Receivables and inventories had to be substantially pared to make Kodak competitive in the digital business.

While the Finance group works most visibly in the Control quadrant of the Wholonics model, the effects of its successes and failures reverberate throughout the organization. For example, financially focused initiatives have been one of the keys to the resurgence of PepsiCo under CEO Roger A. Enrico. Under Enrico, Pepsi has become leaner and more efficient, as capital-intensive non-core businesses such as restaurants and bottling have been spun off. These divestitures have freed up resources, enabling Pepsi to launch a very aggressive marketing campaign to unseat Coca-Cola as number one in the soft-drinks business.

Such success stories raise organizational expectations that others have of the Finance group. Many Finance groups fall short of meeting these expectations, leading to frustration. This chapter examines how the five basic tools of value creation can be applied to Finance.

■ What Does Value Mean to You and Your Organization?

With legions of MBAs now working in the Finance groups of various organizations, the question of what value means to people in Finance would appear to be ridiculously easy to answer. It's all about shareholder value, isn't it? True. But this ready answer masks deeper issues. How does a member of the Finance group *personally* define value? And how does Finance help the rest of the organization to view value creation in a way that actually turns out to maximize shareholder value?

In my experience, Finance sometimes has as hard a time coming to grips with these issues as any other part of the organization. Here is an example.

A few years ago I was discussing with a CFO the role that Finance could play as a strategic partner in his company. He told me about a meeting he had with his CEO to identify the outstanding contributors in the Finance organization for the past year. The CEO had asked the CFO for nominations. The CFO presented two names and described the fine work of each person. The CEO sat quietly for a moment and then shook his head, "These people have done fine work, but they are not leaders. And not what we are looking for." When the meeting ended, the CFO told me, "He just does not understand what we are supposed to do."

In this age of global competition, there is an increasing emphasis on the evolution and growth of the organization. Every function and every executive is expected to provide leadership in terms of increasing organizational responsiveness and growth. Yet, for some disciplines and related functions, this is a particularly difficult challenge. Finance is such an area. People like the CFO I just mentioned are deeply socialized in the logic of regulation and control. These are tools of the Control quadrant. Their background often makes it difficult to understand what people like the CEO in that example are looking for, which typically goes beyond the traditional role played by Finance. In more than one company, this problem is causing financial executives to lose credibility. In fact, in relatively few companies is Finance really providing the kind of analytical and decision support that a focus on growth requires.

To see how Finance perceives its role in value creation, I now report the results of large-sample survey research. These results are summarized in Table 7.1.

Table 7.1. The Role of Finance in Value Creation

What performance metrics do you typically use?	How does your group create value? What are the value drivers you control?	How do you destroy value?	How do the financial goals of the company impede your value creation?	How would you like to redefine these goals?
- Timely, reliable, and value-added financial information - Accurate reports - Least-cost financing (interest cost as a percentage of sales) - Robust internal controls - Performance of earnings forecasts versus analysts' EPS estimates and forecasts - Cost reductions - Asset returns	- Reduce working capital as percentage of sales - Identify and divest non-value-added assets - Achieve reduced interest costs - Improve communications with investors by creating effective new Web site - Cost savings from outsourcing company's 401(K) plan - Speed up conversion of accounts receivables into cash - Implement cost controls	- Countless reconciliations between systems to maintain data reliability due to poor information technology systems - Failure to report significant risks - Excessive routine reporting - Inadequate hedging of risks	- Failure to invest in the right information systems that could increase efficiency	- Include as part of the performance metrics for Finance the effectiveness with which financial information is communicated within the firm and to the financial community - Evaluate on the basis of how fairly priced the company's stock is judged to be

Of all the functional groups surveyed, the responses by members of the Finance group were the most revealing. There are numerous points worth noting.

First, while virtually every other group in the organization viewed the financial goals of the company as being too short-term in orientation and thus sometimes generating value-destroying behavior, people in Finance do not see this orientation as an impediment to value creation. There's no need to judge who is right and who is wrong here—the disparity indicates an interesting disconnect between how Finance views the company's financial goals and how the rest of the organization views them. At the very least, this difference in perceptions may reflect a potentially serious lack of internal communication.

Second, the performance metrics used in practice for judging Finance focus largely on the traditional role of people in this group as reporters of financial information and controllers of costs, expenses, and cash flow—in other words, on the Control quadrant. The data do not paint a picture of Finance as a strategic partner in the business and a comprehensive contributor to the creation and monitoring of value.

Third, Finance does seem to have a clear definition of value, one that revolves around improving cost efficiency and asset productivity. Both are important contributors to shareholder value and essential components of the Control quadrant. However, they provide a remarkably limited perception of the role of Finance in the organization.

Fourth, the three key ways in which Finance views value destruction as being linked to its own actions are (1) an excessive focus on data reconciliations and reporting, (2) failure to adequately recognize and report the risks to which the company is exposed and to manage (hedge) these risks, and (3) failure to invest in the appropriate information systems for managing the company's financial data. Thus, it appears that Finance specialists view an excessive Control quadrant focus, as manifested

□

in reporting and data reconciliations, as destroying value. The solution appears to be to invest appropriately in management information systems. It turns out that effective value creators in Finance take the lead in helping to design such systems and convincing the organization to make the necessary investments.

Finally, of the principal reasons why the understanding of value can get blurred, the functional silo mentality is the most evident in Table 7.1. Much of the perception of how value is created and destroyed has to do narrowly with the activities Finance itself is involved in. There is not much evidence of a comprehensive, cross-functional concept of value creation.

■ Multiple Value-Creation Perspectives

The traditional role of Finance personnel has focused on the Control quadrant of the Wholonics model. The activities that consume their time are reporting information, controlling various costs and related activities, and managing risk.

These are essential activities that will always be a pivotal component of Finance's core mission. But, whether they like it or not, people in this group are increasingly being expected to go beyond these traditional activities and become strategic partners and leaders. Their challenge is that no one else in the organization can tell them how to assume these roles. Finance is uniquely equipped to look out across the entire value chain of the organization—to assess the value-creation tradeoffs in various activities, to see how the pieces all fit together to form a coherent whole, and to provide a perspective that is both appealing to shareholders and responsive to the multiple ways in which value is created by the organization.

The task is formidable indeed, mainly because of four organizational realities that act as impediments: the inability to

communicate effectively, the difficulty of being a strategic partner and leader, the inherent tension between the traditional role
of control and the new role of strategic partner, and the challenge of being a business integrator. It's useful to look at each of
these in turn.

The Inability to Communicate Effectively

Finance is a highly technical discipline, replete with its own ter-
minology, abbreviations, concepts, and jargon. Over time, those
who work in the area become so comfortable with the language
of Finance that thinking and speaking in these terms becomes
second nature. To an outsider—anybody who hasn't been working in Finance—however, the language of the discipline often
seems unintuitive and strange. As one HR manager remarked
to me at the end of a Finance lecture I gave to a cross-functional
group in a company, "You know, this stuff is actually quite interesting when you can see it in simple terms. But this is all the
stuff I carefully avoided in college!" Finance is the lifeblood of
the organization and potentially of great interest everywhere,
but few Finance managers are able to communicate in simple
business terms with the rest of the organization.

The problem is compounded because members of Finance
groups rarely understand the importance of communicating
through visual means and in ways that make learning enjoyable
for the recipients of the communication. It can be done. One
wonderful counter-example that I observed recently was at
Whirlpool, where the Finance group had come up with a picture
called the "EVA Regatta." The picture depicts a sailing ship on
an ocean that is divided into four quadrants separated by ocean
depth, protruding land masses, and so on. The idea is to visualize
that the assets of the company fall into one of the four quadrants:
those that are destroying value (negative Economic Value) and
have a lot of capital invested in them, those that are destroying

value but have modest amounts of capital invested in them, those that are creating value (positive Economic Value) and have modest capital invested in them, and finally, those that are creating value and have substantial capital invested in them. How the company will allocate future resources to a group of assets (a product or a business unit), and thus the direction in which the ship will sail, depends on the quadrant in which these assets lie.

This imaginative illustration provides a nice visual representation of how the company will be allocating resources in the near future. The resulting understanding can become a compass for everybody in the organization to steer by.

A good business presentation follows the compelling logic of what has been called the Pyramid Principle.[1] This approach involves describing the situation first in fairly brief terms, identifying the factors that complicate the situation, delineating the key questions that are raised by the situation and its complication, and then presenting the final recommendations as answers to these questions—and producing each part of the pyramid briskly enough to keep the audience awake. The recommendations show up very early in the presentation, around the third of fourth slide, and all supporting details are presented afterwards to justify and support them. Unfortunately, far too many presentations by Finance managers take the opposite approach. Mind-numbing details are presented first and the rest of the presentation unfolds like a mystery novel, with the audience made to wait until the very end to hear the recommendations that become the "punch line"!

Many companies have come to recognize the important role of improving communication with the Finance group. One company I work with, The Limited, decided to launch a training program specifically to address this issue. The new CFO, Ann Hailey, decided to have a series of one-day programs in which business-unit CFOs, directors of Finance, and other key personnel came together in groups of twelve to fifteen to go through concept discussions and a structured set of exercises designed to develop proficiency in the logic of business presentations. I have been involved in taking numerous groups through the program, and more groups are scheduled for the future.

The Difficulty of Being a Strategic Partner and Leader

Finance, like many other functions within the organization, evolves over time, going through four phases. In the first phase, Finance is more or less a reporting function, with the Controller concentrating on producing financial reports for internal consumption and the Treasurer handling reports to the external financial community. As the organization grows in size, Finance enters a second phase in which the task of designing and implementing various control mechanisms becomes as important as the reporting function. Costs and expenses of various sorts as well as risks are tracked, controlled, and reported. Much of what was summarized in Table 7.1 suggests a heavy focus on these traditional reporting and controlling tasks.

As the complexity of the business grows and the relevant information about the business becomes extremely fragmented, Finance enters the third phase. Now it is called upon to analyze these diverse pieces of information and help to provide a unifying shareholder-value perspective for decision making. This function requires a deep understanding of the business so that effective decision-support analysis can be provided. Developing multiple value creation perspectives becomes an imperative.

The fourth and final stage of the evolution of Finance takes it beyond the realm of analysis to strategic partnership. This role calls for skills in presentation and persuasion. Finance has to take its analysis, present it effectively to others, explain its ramifications for decisions, and be persuasive in having decisions made that are consonant with maximizing shareholder wealth.

This evolution of the Finance function reflects the evolution of organizations themselves from vertical hierarchies—built in the days when mass manufacturing driven by economies of scale was king—to the flatter, cross-functional, process-driven organizations of the present day, where customer focus, speed, and adaptiveness are essential. The adaptive organization requires Finance to develop a more effective cross-functional dialogue with various groups within the organization—and to be the group that melds these diverse viewpoints into a single but constantly shifting perspective about the decisions that should drive the organization forward. Figure 7.1 shows this pattern of development.

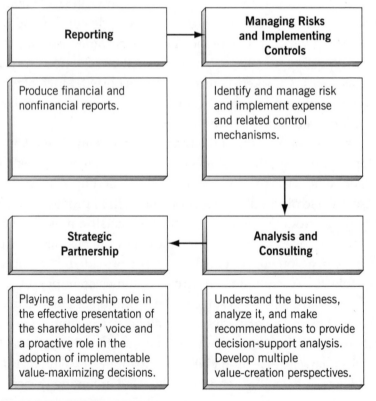

Reporting

Produce financial and nonfinancial reports.

Managing Risks and Implementing Controls

Identify and manage risk and implement expense and related control mechanisms.

Strategic Partnership

Playing a leadership role in the effective presentation of the shareholders' voice and a proactive role in the adoption of implementable value-maximizing decisions.

Analysis and Consulting

Understand the business, analyze it, and make recommendations to provide decision-support analysis. Develop multiple value-creation perspectives.

Figure 7.1. The Evolution of Finance

Some Finance organizations I know of have evolved to the third phase. That is, they have people who have developed good skills in analysis. Some are even good consultants. But these groups are few compared to those that have merely mastered the skills needed in the first two phases.

Rarest of all, though, is the Finance organization that has truly evolved to the fourth phase. Part of the reason that such development is difficult is the perception that those in Finance themselves have about their own role. There are many in Finance who will tell you that it is not their job to play that role. Rather, conducting financial analysis and recommending solutions for others to implement is where their role ends.

This is a classic staff support mind-set. It is very difficult for people in Finance to be effective guardians of the voice of the shareholder if they limit their role to that of consultants whose assignment is over when the report summarizing the recommendations is handed to the internal client.

The other reason why evolving to the fourth phase is a formidable challenge is that others in the organization also typically perceive the role of Finance as being limited to the first three phases. As a result a Finance person who attempts to be proactive in decision implementation will often be viewed as stepping out of line and is likely to be pushed back.

The Tension Between the Traditional Role of Control and the New Role of Strategic Partnership

Of all the so-called staff support disciplines, Finance perhaps has the most difficult challenge in becoming a strategic partner with other groups in the organization because control is such an important part of its responsibilities. This task requires monitoring the financial transactions that occur within the organization. The very term *control* seems directly opposed to *partnership*. Partnership belongs to the Collaborate quadrant of the Wholonics model. Control obviously is a different quadrant.

Very few people in Finance have effectively come to grips with this inherent and unavoidable tension. Part of the reason is that partnership has a negative zone too. Taken too far, partnership detracts sufficiently from the control function of Finance so that Finance fails in its most basic mission. By the same token, however, control taken too far makes partnership impossible. The challenge is to figure out where and how to strike the appropriate balance.

The Challenge of Being a Business Integrator

In a small organization, all key decision makers have all the information they need. However, in large organizations this is not possible. Information must necessarily fragment to ensure that people are able to concentrate on the information that is most important to their jobs.

An illustration of this difference is provided by the "line and circle experiment," designed by organizational psychologist Alex Bavelas.[2] In this experiment, one group of participants is arranged in a straight line with each person allowed to talk only to one person, the head of the group. This straight line arrangement is supposed to mimic a hierarchical organization structure in which the hierarchy dictates communication lines. The other group of participants is arranged in a circle. All the participants in the second group are allowed to communicate with their immediate neighbors, in the spirit of participative management. Each participant is given a box containing an assortment of marbles. The group's task is to identify one color that is common to all the boxes given to members of that group.

It turns out that when the marbles are relatively simple in color and design—all solid colors—the line arrangement does better than the circle. But when the marbles become more complex in their color patterns—with mottled designs and various colors in each marble—the circle does better than the line. Because each person in the circle group can talk to the next person rather than just the leader, the group is able to adapt more quickly to the complexity of the task.

This is often used as a justification for participative management. However, a lesser-known finding of this research is that when all lines of communication were open—when participants could not only talk to the person next to them but to all other members of the group—then the problem-solving ability of the circle group diminished significantly. In fact, the group became almost paralyzed.

The lesson from this experiment is that in large organizations there is an optimal level of communication. More is not always better. Thus, you may need to limit communication and the information made available to various groups for reasons of efficiency, not secrecy. The inevitable result is a fragmentation of information.

Any fragmentation creates a need for *integration.* This is a key responsibility of the Finance group. As indicated earlier, Finance is uniquely equipped to provide this integration because it has the ability to look out across the entire value chain and comprehend what any initiative means for value creation for the entire organization. Finance should hear the voice of the shareholder most clearly.

The importance of such integration has recently been emphasized in different contexts. For example, an extensive study completed by the Wharton Financial Services Research Center[3] found that what drives performance in banking is the alignment of information technology, human resource management, and capital investments with an appropriate production technology. The study concludes, "To achieve this alignment, banks need to invest in a cadre of 'organizational architects' that are capable of integrating these varied pieces together to form a coherent structure."

These four roadblocks are both a diagnosis of the reasons for the failure of Finance to be an effective value creator and a prescription for success. By dealing effectively with its built-in roadblocks, Finance can indeed become an effective business integrator, strategic partner, and leader. This transition involves an evolution in the Wholonics profile in the direction depicted in Figure 7.2.

Implied in the desired profile shown in Figure 7.2 is that Finance has to become more proactive in helping the organization to grow. The traditional role of Finance was to assume that the "top line" of the Income Statement (sales revenue) was someone else's responsibility, and then focus on how to improve the "bottom line" (net income). This naturally focused all of the energy of Finance personnel on cost containment and the two lower quadrants of the Wholonics model. But as business integrators, Finance people are expected to play an active role in the Create quadrant. This task is inherently difficult because the Cre-

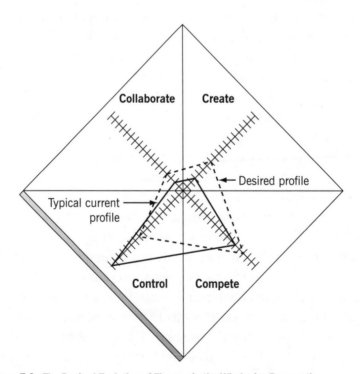

Figure 7.2. The Desired Evolution of Finance in the Wholonics Perspective

ate and Control quadrants are diagonally opposite from each other. Operating in the Create quadrant is difficult for Finance groups and can even be a source of great discomfort, but it can also be a source of strength if they manage to master it. Further, Finance must begin to play an active role in the Collaborate quadrant, helping the organization structure itself to maximize value creation. Organization design, a traditional HR domain, must now be part of Finance's portfolio of competencies. To see why, take a look at the following case study.

Finance-Driven Reorganization: Reuters

The British news agency and technology company Reuters is a global player at the conjunction of three industries: information and news, information technology, and financial services. Its role in information and news is well known. In information technology and financial services, it is a provider of software to financial service firms, and it also owns Instinet, an electronic trading system.

Reuters was an outstanding success over decades, and one of the favorites of stock market analysts ever since it went public in 1984. However, in the mid-to-late 1990s, its growth slowed and analysts began to question the company's strategy.

One of the major issues for analysts was the apparent lack of transparency when they wanted to examine the company's financial performance. The problem was that the company was organized by geography rather than product. This meant not only that the reporting lines of authority within the company were defined by geographic regions, but also that financial information was aggregated and reported on a geographic basis. It was difficult for an external analyst to know how well a particular product or business unit was doing, since products were typically sold in many regions and each region sold many products. Analysts were thus hampered in their ability to make product-specific forecasts. This lack of transparency seemed to be adversely affecting the company's stock price—when people have a hard time figuring something out, they tend to assume the worst.

This feedback from the financial community to the company's senior management and Finance organization eventually convinced CEO Peter Job and his executive team to fundamentally reorganize the company. In 1998 the company was reorganized along product lines, a move that was well received by the external financial community.

■ What Is Your Business Strategy?

Finance is intimately involved in implementing the organizational strategy because strategy drives the allocation of resources, and Finance is the resource gatekeeper of the organization. Finance's role in this respect has two implications. First, Finance must be involved in all aspects of strategy—not just in implementing it but in formulating it as well. Second, the challenge for Finance is to design its own strategy so that the implementation of the corporate strategy will maximize value creation. In particular, Finance must help guide the rest of the organization about ways to implement the company strategy.

This section presents two case studies that illustrate how Finance can play its people strategic role. The first involves designing a strategy to create value by shrinking or downsizing. The second involves designing a strategy to create value by growing.

Less Is More: General Dynamics

In 1991, defense contractor General Dynamics engaged a new management team and instructed it to maximize shareholder value.[4] At that time the defense contracting industry in general was faced with declining demand and excess capacity projections. Many firms responded by making defense-related acquisitions and diversifying into nondefense businesses. But General Dynamics chose to focus on shareholder value and undertook many painful initiatives in anticipation of forthcoming problems instead of waiting until the problems were at the company's doorstep, as is usually the case. How General Dynamics managed to do this illustrates the way a company and its Finance organization can excel in the Compete quadrant.

The origins of General Dynamics can be traced back to 1899, when it began as the Electric Boat Company. It became a major supplier of submarines and cargo ships to the U.S. Navy during both World Wars. By 1960, it was a major manufacturer of aircraft, booster rockets, and missiles, and it dominated the nuclear submarine business. It was around this time that it was renamed General Dynamics.

Over the next three decades the company grew impressively, fueled in part by its foreign sales. Its products included the F16 jet fighter, the M-1 and M-60 Abrams tanks, and eventually civilian aircraft (a capability it acquired as a result of purchasing Cessna).

On September 27, 1989, the company announced the hiring of William Anders as CEO. Anders was a former air force pilot and *Apollo 8* astronaut who had orbited the moon during Christmas 1968. At the time the appointment was announced, defense contracting was a growth industry. Anders was scheduled to become CEO on January 1, 1991.

Between the announcement of his appointment and actually taking over as CEO, Anders saw the outlook for the industry change dramatically. The Soviet Union disintegrated in 1990 and the Berlin Wall fell the same year, signaling the end of the Cold War. By the time Anders took the helm, the forecast of a reduced demand for General Dynamics products was as plain as the proverbial writing on the wall.

As soon as he stepped up to the plate, Anders made it very clear that his goal was to transform General Dynamics into a shareholder-value-driven enterprise. His strategy included these main points:

- Increase returns on assets
- Improve product profit margins
- Focus more sharply on investments

What followed was as fundamental a transformation of an organization as almost any in recent corporate history.

Anders's constructive assault on General Dynamics was two-pronged. First, he put in place an organizational change plan that involved changing mind-sets, incentives, knowledge, and behavior. Second, he implemented a shareholder-value-focused strategy for the company.

The organizational change plan had five principal elements. First, a new management team was appointed. Eighteen of the top twenty-five executives were either new to General Dynamics or new to their positions. Second, Anders invited a Wall Street analyst to alert top management and directors to the severity of the company's situation. The analyst noted that the company's Price/Earnings (P/E) ratio ranked 497th in the S&P 500—a sobering reminder of the stock market's assessment of the company's future growth potential.

Third, Anders promoted James Mellor, who had been executive vice president in charge of submarines, tanks, and overseas sales, to president and chief operating officer. Anders described Mellor's role as follows:

> We talked a lot about focusing on shareholder value and each
> of our top executives was committed to this objective. Even
> though that was our *focus,* it was not our *strategy* because
> maximize shareholder value is difficult to operationalize. Mellor
> really helped the managers understand how to run their busi-
> nesses. Just accepting the idea of shareholder value isn't enough.
> For a lot of the managers, it was a case of "OK, I believe in
> shareholder value, but what should I do tomorrow?" Mellor
> taught them how to manage for cash.

Fourth, the company was divided into business areas, and decision-making authority was pushed further down into the hierarchy. To help managers to adjust to their newly expanded roles, Mellor asked a top business school to develop a special one-week seminar for 150 of the company's managers. The seminar covered business basics and investment analysis so that General Dynamics managers would "think like business people, not aerospace engineers."

Fifth, to focus his management team on maximizing shareholder value, Anders reengineered the company's executive compensation system. All links to accounting measures of performance were eliminated. Compensation was tied to the General Dynamics stock price through stock options, and incentives were provided for employees to hold on to their stock positions. Under the plan, twenty-five top executives would receive approximately 1.5 percent of the increase in shareholder value for the first $10 increase in stock price and 3 percent for subsequent 10 percent increases in stock price. And unlike many incentive compensation plans, *the plan did not impose any limit on the amount of bonuses as long as the stock price continued to increase.*

The new management compensation plan was not without its detractors. The company's unionized workforce was openly critical. Many were outraged that senior executives could earn large bonuses while the rank and file were being laid off. Compensation consultant Graef Crystal voiced his criticism as follows: "This is a case of a guy getting lots of money, and he's an island of prosperity in a sea of misery."[5] Crystal also said, "The CEO of General Dynamics must be the laziest man in the world. Look at all the incentive plans they have to give him to go to work in the morning."[6]

While the emotion behind such criticism is understandable, it has little economic merit. To Anders's credit, he persisted despite the criticism. Anders also defined a new strategy for the company. His strategy had the following three elements.

First, the company would eschew diversification into nondefense businesses. In line with this, General Dynamics announced in October 1997 that its largest nondefense subsidiary, Cessna Aircraft, was for sale. Moreover, the company said it would study all of its nondefense operations as possible divestiture candidates.

Second, Anders provided industry leadership by publicly urging the industry to both downsize and consolidate. His mantra was: "No one should invest and grow in the defense industry."

Third, like General Electric, General Dynamics announced that it would remain only in businesses where it could both be #1 or #2 and achieve a "critical mass" to justify dedicated factories. Anders identified four businesses within the company's "core capabilities" that passed these two tests—military aircraft, nuclear submarines, tanks, and space systems. He then announced a formal plan of contraction in which the company would seek to sell units outside these four areas.

As a consequence of implementing this strategy, General Dynamics sales decreased 66 percent from $9.5 billion in 1991 to $3.2 billion in 1993. Anders remarked, "Although human and physical assets would ultimately have to leave the industry, GD's assets were in general being consolidated into other companies."

Even before the results of the company's organizational change plan and strategy were known, three Wall Street firms put General Dynamics on their "buy list." Why? Because of the new incentive plan focusing on shareholder wealth, the reduced capital and R&D spending, and the possibility of stock repurchases to return cash to shareholders.

By the time Anders had been in his job as CEO for about three years, spectacular shareholder value had been created. Every $100 invested in General Dynamics in January 1991, when Anders came on board, was worth $653 by December 1993, including cash and dividend reinvestments. Over this time, the value-weighted defense industry portfolio (excluding General Dynamics) was worth $214 per original $100 and the S&P 500 was worth $155.

The market value of General Dynamics equity was $1 billion in January 1991. By December 1993, it was $4.5 billion. The company had shrunk to a third of its size in terms of sales and had grown four and a half times in terms of the market value of its equity. Somewhere between $2.3 billion and $3.5 billion of the company's market value of equity was directly attributable to management actions under Anders.

What are the key lessons to learn from this case?

First, as exciting as growth is, there are times when creating value means downsizing. When a company finds itself in such a situation, Finance has to take the lead in coming up with the right strategy and making others in the organization bite the bullet. Helping the company make difficult decisions is an important aspect of functioning effectively in the Compete quadrant.

Second, aligning executive compensation with shareholder value is essential. In fact, it is a crime against those who own the business to not do so. As Anders noted:

> When we started to build a new management team, we wanted *partners*, not high-salaried people . . . to attract good people and to change behavior, you have to compensate them well.

I didn't want to take the company private, but I wanted a private-company mentality. I wanted to break out of the "hired hand" mentality. There is an enormous difference between being a smart hired hand and being a partner.

Executive compensation that is closely tied either to stock price or to identifiable drivers of stock price can be a powerful instrument of positive organizational change. It is as much the responsibility of Finance as it is of HR to take part in designing and implementing of such a compensation plan.

Third, no one should assume that people understand what shareholder value really means when they say that they will focus all of their efforts on maximizing it. Just providing an executive compensation plan linked to shareholder value is not enough. Most managers have only a hazy understanding of what maximizing shareholder value means for their day-to-day decision making. Executive education and constant communication are the only ways to combat this problem. In this respect, the role Mellor played at General Dynamics was pivotal.

Fourth, there is a crucial difference between the politics and the economics of executive compensation. If you provide incentives to create value under excess capacity, these incentives invariably direct executives to shed this excess, so it is unavoidable that you pay bonuses to senior executives during layoffs.

One might argue that the high payments to senior executives will adversely affect employee morale. For example, employees at the General Dynamics San Diego plant carried placards reading, "No Bogus Bonus for Bill," referring to the CEO. However, I suspect that the low morale among rank-and-file employees was due less to Anders's compensation than to the dim prospects for the defense industry. If you're not convinced, consider the following questions:

- Would employee morale have been higher if Anders had worked for free?

- Why isn't employee morale low at Disney, where CEO Michael Eisner's total compensation in 1998 was reported to be $580 million?
- Could senior management at General Dynamics have made the gut-wrenching layoff and asset divestiture decisions that they made without the high-powered incentives provided by their compensation contracts?

While it is the task of Finance to help the organization shrink to create value during times of industry decline, it is also the task of Finance to help the organization grow to create value during times of potential industry growth. The following case study illustrates this point.

Sometimes More Is Even More: Wal-Mart

As is well known, Wal-Mart created enormous shareholder value in the 1980s and early 1990s by embarking on a massive expansion coupled with outstanding asset productivity. However, growth began to slow down in the mid-1990s because of intense competition and market saturation. The first quarter of 1996 saw the first drop in quarterly earnings in twenty-five years.

Wal-Mart faced two major problems that pulled it in opposite directions. First, customers were not spending enough in stores. Second, there was too much capital tied up because of high SKU complexity. This SKU complexity arose from the desire to customize product offerings to customers' needs. The dilemma was that reducing SKU complexity would threaten "top-line" growth if it led to a decline in sales. Indeed, growing sales demanded more SKU complexity, not less. The Finance group had a tough time simultaneously addressing growth objectives and financial targets, while the Marketing group was unwilling to budge on the SKU complexity issue. As John Percival of the Wharton School noted, "Meaningful dialogue between Finance and Marketing takes place in amazingly few companies. Often times you are faced with the dilemma: do we want to grow or do we want margins? The traditional answer of companies is 'yes'."[7] What did Wal-Mart CFO John B. Menzer do? For starters, he first went to the group that presented the problem—Marketing. His approach was to ask two simple questions: How can we serve the customer better? What is the evidence that the present degree of customization is necessary or helping us to sell more and make higher profits?

Menzer discovered that there was no model of optimal SKU capacity. Furthermore, there was insufficient information to develop and deploy such a model effectively. These findings led him to take four steps.

First, he decided to conduct better customer research. This research revealed that the company's policy of standardizing SKUs across stores on a national basis was standing in the way of a proper resolution of the complexity issues. The policy was designed to make the whole system more efficient. However, the product needs of stores varied greatly by location. For example, stores in largely Hispanic neighborhoods in Los Angeles had a higher demand for brightly colored products than those in other locations. Carrying SKUs of such products across the entire system was inefficient from an inventory management standpoint, but not carrying them would cost the company sales in some Los Angeles stores.

The solution was to relax the inventory standardization policy so that there would be SKUs specific to stores in a given region. Inventories of those SKUs would not be carried on a national basis. The variety of SKUs available at individual stores was thus expanded as smaller sets of customized product offerings were offered at those stores, while at the same time inventory was lowered across the entire system.

Second, Menzer deemphasized straight financial metrics. Instead metrics were developed for divisions that were tied to the "strategic planks" of the divisional business plans, for example, customer value, distribution and inventory, training, and financial results.

Third, he initiated efforts to tie management compensation to return on Net Assets as a precursor to adopting a "Balanced Scorecard," which is basically a portfolio of measures that apply to various activities like attending to customer satisfaction, satisfying the company's bottom-line objectives, attending to innovation, and so on.

Finally, Menzer initiated the development of a more refined management information system that blended the company's own sophisticated sales data and forecasts with those of vendors to produce a best-of-the-best distribution and replenishment system based on a single, unified forecast. This went a step beyond the existing vendor-managed inventory model in which key suppliers had ready access to the company's product sales figures in order to make timely shipments of replacement products.

The outcome of Menzer's efforts was that Wal-Mart was reenergized and refocused on creating shareholder value. It's not surprising that John Menzer was named one of the winners of the 1999 CFO Excellence Awards.[8]

There are at least four important lessons to be learned from the Wal-Mart case. First, Finance has an important role to play in helping the organization grow. Growth is a Create quadrant activity, and Finance is viewed typically as a discipline that lives in the Control quadrant, which is diagonally opposite. Finance has to find creative solutions to the dilemma that confronts every growing organization: *How do you grow without overutilizing capital?* After all, growing by throwing capital at every growth idea in sight is easy, but it does not create value. The Wal-Mart case shows growth can be achieved in a value-enhancing manner if Finance and Marketing collaborate in developing a value-creation strategy.

Second, as a business integrator, Finance must understand that the group that is apparently creating the problem—Marketing with its fondness for SKU complexity, in Wal-Mart's case—is typically also the source of the solution. Wal-Mart would probably not have discovered the correct approach to solving the problem had Finance not chosen to take the customer as the starting point for analyzing the situation. In other words, Finance had to understand a traditional marketing domain.

Third, the solution to a behavior and business problem often lies in the performance measurement system. At Wal-Mart the Finance organization recognized this and addressed it.

Finally, Finance at Wal-Mart acted in a fully integrated manner with business operations. The group focused on capital and broke the business down into its component pieces to determine where value was being created.

■ What Is Your Personal Measure of Success?

People in the Finance group face two challenges in defining their personal measures of success. First, as Table 7.1 indicates, their traditional orientation is in the value measures of the Control quadrant, which is too limited a value-creation perspective. They must develop a broader, more comprehensive value-creation measure. Second, the consequences of sunflower management are perhaps the most damaging in Finance. Personal measures of success in this group should be very attentive to minimizing it. The following case study illustrates these challenges.

The Politics of Evaluating an Acquisition

A few years ago, I was involved in a consulting assignment with a global company that was considering an acquisition in Asia. The regional financial analyst in Asia had conducted what appeared to be a thorough financial analysis of the proposed acquisition and had forwarded it to the corporate Mergers and Acquisitions (M&A) group for final approval.

However, when the M&A group "ran the numbers," a problem was discovered in the regional analyst's spreadsheets. After the error was corrected, the revised valuation of the proposed acquisition was 20 percent below the original valuation.

The head of the M&A group immediately called the president of the company's Asian operations to alert him to the problem. Unfortunately, this call happened to come the day before final negotiations to acquire the target firm were to begin. The president of Asian operations had already met with the target company's managers and had discussed a tentative acquisition price with them. This tentative price was based on the original (flawed) analysis. It would have been terribly embarrassing for the president of Asian operations to have to revise the price at this late stage. The target firm might well have viewed such a move as a hardball negotiating ploy and backed off.

The regional president reacted with predictable anger when the head of M&A called him. His tirade made three points. First, he accused the M&A group of being oblivious to the company's strategic business needs in Asia. How could the president execute the regional growth strategy at the ridiculously low acquisition price the M&A group had come up with? Second, he challenged the validity of the M&A group's financial analysis. He refused to accept that his own analyst had made a mistake. There must be something not quite right about what the M&A group had done. And finally, even if the M&A group was right, this was a hell of a surprise to dump on the regional president on the eve of his final negotiations!

Eventually, the head of M&A capitulated. The acquisition was completed at the higher price that had been calculated by the region.

What does this case demonstrate? Three lessons stand out.

First, a major difficulty was that the corporate M&A group was invited to the party too late. Why were they looking at the financial analysis when the deal was all but done? Had they been involved earlier, it is possible that they could have had a more constructive dialogue with the president of Asian operations and perhaps changed his mind.

Second, the tradition in this company was for M&A to play a purely advisory role. The regional president thus expected the group to simply rubber-stamp and validate for record-keeping purposes what he felt was the right decision all along. He did not expect a dissenting voice.

This second point is reminiscent of another company I worked with where capital appropriation requests were often sent to the Finance group for "approval" and sign-off well after the capital had already been invested! A powerful executive vice president in this company once said to me: "I know the needs of my business unit better than anyone else in this company. Why should I have to wait interminably for those bureaucrats in Finance to sign off on my capital appropriation requests? All that they do is slow the process down when market conditions demand that I move quickly."

Third, the eventual behavior of the head of M&A validated what the regional president thought about the M&A group. The M&A head acted in a purely advisory manner, pointing out a problem but backing off from the right decision in the face of stern opposition.

Why did the head of M&A behave like this? *Because he was a manager, not a leader.* A manager measures success on the basis of personal survival. A leader measures success on the basis of vision realization. A manager's source of power is effectiveness at completing transactions, which in turn requires political astuteness and the right compromises. A leader's source of power is core values. A manager's orientation to authority is to be responsive. A leader is self-authorizing. A manager's source of satisfaction is approval by others. A leader's source of satisfaction emanates internally and is related to how effectively the vision was realized. In short, a leader is an internally driven person who cares enough to bring differentiation to the organization. A leader continually breaks others out of the status quo and introduces variations to the system. These variations allow the system to grow and adapt.

It takes a leader to evolve to the phase of strategic partnership and leadership described earlier. Such evolution requires that the truth can never be compromised. As an astute corporate treasurer remarked to me, "It is the job of the Finance person to tell the truth." This may sound a bit like motherhood and apple pie. But it is also profoundly true. Having the true voice of the shareholder heard at all times is the raison d'être of the Finance organization.

At this juncture in the discussion, the pragmatist usually objects. "But what could the head of M&A have done in this case? He tried everything he could. The regional president, who outranked him in the corporate hierarchy, simply would not listen." The fact of the matter is that the head of M&A did *not* do everything he could. Knowing that the company was about to overpay by millions of dollars, he could have talked his boss, the CEO, into overruling the regional president. He could have offered to resign if this was not done. None of this would have endeared him to the regional president. None of it would have facilitated his personal survival in the organization. None of it would have been part of the way good managers behave in organizations. But that is what leaders do—routinely!

Leadership has an honest quality about it that people begin to appreciate and accept over time. Honesty may not be the fastest path to popularity, but it does command respect and is remarkably effective in bringing about organizational change.

For people in Finance, personal measures of success need to include the extent to which they become effective business integrators and leaders. That means forsaking sunflower management in order to focus the organization more sharply on value creation. Further, being an effective business integrator requires interacting with many different groups within the company, some of whom may pay lip service to the value of an initiative but really fail to see its importance. A business integrator must have the skills to identify these potential roadblocks and understand how to make it in the interest of these blockers themselves to cooperate in making the initiative a success. In this endeavor, persistence is essential. New initiatives almost always engender resistance in the organization. Having a clear value-driven measure of success and clinging to that vision can help one remain persistent in the face of inevitable resistance.

■ Developing Speed

No one in Finance needs to be convinced about the importance of speed in value creation. Speed is an essential ingredient of the Compete quadrant, which is a quadrant in which many progressive Finance groups are already positioned.

Knowing the importance of speed is not the same as knowing how to maximize it, however. The latter requires an understanding of how to improve the *flexibility* of the organization in exploiting growth opportunities quickly and without committing excessive resources. Among the many challenges facing Finance is that growth often requires making highly risky investments, yet limiting risk and the size of investments is usually a key aspect of optimizing value creation. As a result, companies often either plunge into strategically important and risky investments that end up destroying value or avoid these investments altogether. The latter course sometimes results in slowing the organization down and conceding valuable territory to competitors. How can this paradox be resolved?

One nice illustration of how to cope with this tension is provided by General Electric's growth strategy in the home appliance business.

Running Along a High Wire: GE Appliances

In the early 1990s GE Appliances, like many other Western appliance companies, viewed China as a major growth opportunity. Its initial plan was to build large manufacturing facilities in China to feed all markets in Asia—a kind of "Pan Asian" strategy.[9]

So in early 1992, GE Appliances sent one of its Marketing vice presidents, Bruce Albertson, to locate appropriate Chinese joint venture (JV) partners for manufacturing. Albertson came back with a number of possibilities. The fly in the ointment, however, was that GE had a minimum 20 percent rate-of-return-on-capital constraint that none of these possibilities was able to satisfy. This led to initial friction between Finance and Marketing and between the central office and the region.

Eventually, it dawned on the decision makers at GE Appliances that no Chinese manufacturing JV was going to be financially acceptable. And yet being in China was a strategic priority.

The cognitive breakthrough that solved the problem was the recognition that a strategy of having a significant presence in China did not necessarily mean *manufacturing* in China. The biggest hurdle most Western companies face in China is logistics. The distribution system there is nowhere close to being as well developed as it is in North America or Western Europe. To address this problem, GE Appliances signed a JV agreement with a national sales distributor. And to deal with the financial constraints related to manufacturing, it decided to outsource all manufacturing of appliances in China.

This outsourcing was a break from tradition for GE, which prided itself on its manufacturing excellence. GE called this departure from its original plan a "smart bombing" strategy, indicating that a one-size-fits-all approach would not be right for all its products. Of course, the company then had to deal with issues related to training its JV partner in manufacturing techniques to assure the desired product quality.

These issues, however, were dealt with. The important point is that GE had to commit *no* capital to manufacturing in China. This allowed it to move forward quickly and without adding potentially unproductive assets. As the dynamics of the appliance industry in China and the rest of Asia evolved during the 1990s, the wisdom of GE's strategy become apparent. Being freed of the constraint to generate enough profit to cover the capital charge associated with investments in manufacturing assets, GE Appliances was apparently the only Western appliance manufacturer to generate positive Economic Value in China from the beginning.

What GE Appliances did in China is a classic illustration of how Finance can use a "real options" approach to resolve the tension between the strategic imperative to grow and the financial constraint that returns on investments must be above some hurdle rate. A financial option entitles option holders to either buy or sell a share stock at a predetermined (strike) price. Option holders have the *option* to buy or sell—they don't have to do so. Because of this, the value of the option increases as the riskiness of the underlying stock increases.

Real investments like GE's foray into China also often have option-like characteristics. Since investments in China are likely to be very risky, options on those investments are very valuable. The strategic implication is that one's investment strategy in such a risky environment should be designed to create options rather than extinguish or exercise them. GE Appliances' strategy of outsourcing its manufacturing created the option to make manufacturing investments in the future. Had GE gone into China with full-scale manufacturing facilities, it would have exercised its manufacturing options. And that would not have been as valuable for its shareholders as its outsourcing strategy.

In other words, risky investment opportunities require exploratory investments that allow the firm to establish a toehold in the market without exposing a lot of its capital to risk. Making these investments also permits the firm to learn how to operate effectively in the new market. If what it learns reveals that further investments are warranted, it can exercise its options and invest larger amounts of capital. If it learns that further investments are not warranted, it can choose to let its options expire unexercised.[10]

This kind of approach has also been used by Wal-Mart. In 1998 it opened "experimental" grocery stores in Arkansas. Each store would be 40,000 square feet, the same size as traditional supermarkets. This is a classic real-options strategy. If the experimental stores are successful, then Wal-Mart will make a stronger push into the grocery market, a highly fragmented $415 billion business that the company could dominate. If what Wal-Mart learns about the grocery business discourages it from committing further capital, its losses will be relatively small. Either way, the company will not have to tolerate the delays that usually accompany extensive market research and feasibility studies. Speed is enhanced—and with limited commitment of resources.

One obstacle that many firms face in developing an options approach to Create quadrant initiatives is that their traditional value-creation model has depended greatly on scale economies and mass manufacturing. The option approach, by contrast, calls for small plays with very limited production. This strategy requires a fundamentally different mind-set.

■ Organizational Success Strategies for Finance

There are many outstanding Finance groups that are sources of competitive advantage for their organizations. These Finance groups have done a thorough job of convincing their organizations that value creation should be their singular focus and that the organization should be guided by a single, clear definition of value—without compromise or apology. Here is a case study of a company that has done a fine job of achieving this focus.

Shareholder Value Via Customer Satisfaction: Diageo

Diageo is one of the world's leading consumer goods companies. Based in the United Kingdom, it was formed in December 1997 through the merger of GrandMet and Guinness. Its products consist of brand-name foods and drinks, including Smirnoff, Johnnie Walker, J&B, Gordon's, Pillsbury, Häagen-Dazs, Guinness, and Burger King.

In its 1998 annual report, Diageo states its objective as follows:

Diageo is in business to create value for our shareholders by delighting our consumers all around the world. Diageo's long-term goal is to be in the top five of a group of 20 of the world's leading consumer goods companies in terms of the total return we generate for our shareholders.

As CEO John McGrath states, "My job is simple. It's to make sure that everyone in this company is obsessed with delighting our consumers and creating value for our shareholders."

To measure the company's progress in achieving its objective, it has adopted Economic Value (which Diageo refers to as "Economic Profit") as both a performance metric and its unambiguous measure of value. Diageo calls its core business philosophy "managing for value" and "about having the creativity and commitment to make sure that all our decisions maximize value for our shareholders." It explains why it adopted this measure:

Why is economic profit a good measure?

- Economic profit tells you about value creation—the most important issue for the shareholder.
- Earnings per share and profit before interest and tax don't take account of the balance sheet, so they don't measure returns on invested capital.
- Growth in turnover may mask the fact that increased volume doesn't necessarily mean increased value for shareholders—sometimes the opposite.

What is impressive about Diageo is its very clear definition of value and how it is to be measured. Moreover, in CEO McGrath's statement, it is also clear that although value is to be measured this way, it is to be created by achieving the highest level of customer satisfaction. Although Diageo's strategy is sharply focused on growth, the company is careful to point out that it is only interested in growth that creates shareholder value.

It's now possible to pull together the ideas developed in this chapter to present a model of organizational success for Finance. This is done in Figure 7.3.

■ Personal Success Strategies for Finance

At the personal level, people in Finance need to do four things. First, assess honestly which of the four phases of Finance development described earlier in the chapter (reporting, control, providing a unified perspective, and strategic partnership) you occupy in your own development. Use your assessment to

What Does Value Mean? Identifying the Value Drivers	Develop Multiple Value-Creation Perspectives
• Convince the rest of the organization about the benefit of a single-minded focus on creating shareholder value. • Master the tools of the Control and Compete quadrants that help you be proficient in the traditional tasks of reporting, control, and cost and asset productivity. • Expand your competencies to include expertise in Create quadrant skills. Help the organization grow.	• Become an effective business integrator by interacting effectively with other groups in the organization, understanding the entire value chain, having conviction about shareholder value, and being persistent. • Learn to communicate effectively, using visual communication and avoiding jargon. • Learn how to resolve the inherent tension between strategic partnership and control. • Develop competencies in the Create and Compete quadrants that go beyond your traditional competencies. Help design your company's organization structure to optimize value creation.

Speed	Develop Appropriate Strategy and Measures of Success
• Help the organization adopt management information systems that improve decision-making speed. • Use real options in investments to help the organization operate effectively in the Create quadrant.	• Be involved in strategy from design to implementation. • Become a leader and develop a personal measure of success that focuses on vision realization rather than personal survival. • Develop a passionate conviction to tell the truth and defend the interests of the shareholders.

Figure 7.3. How Finance Can Optimize Value Creation

determine what you need to work on in order to evolve into an effective strategic partner and a leader.

Second, your strong quadrants are supposed to be Control and Compete. Control is a traditional strength and Compete an emerging strength. Consequently, your accounting and financial analysis skills must be top-notch. Stay abreast of the latest developments. Make sure you are constantly educating yourself about the cutting-edge tools of financial analysis.

Third, expand your horizon by developing Collaborate and Create quadrant skills. Make friends with your fellow employees in HR and Marketing. What are their concerns? How can they help you? How can you help them?

Finally, develop the mind-set of a transformational leader rather than a transactional manager. Develop a passionate conviction for the truth and for an organizational focus on shareholder value.

CHAPTER SUMMARY

In this chapter I have explored the five secrets of value creators in the context of Finance. The meaning of value in Finance often gets interpreted in classic Control quadrant terms—reporting financial information through the organizational hierarchy and controlling costs and processes. The development of multiple value-creation perspectives and positioning Finance more effectively in the Collaborate and Create quadrants is particularly difficult because Finance has to wear the two conflicting hats of strategic partnership and control.

On the issue of strategy, the role of Finance as a business integrator means that it is uniquely equipped to both help formulate and then implement the strategy. In helping with strategy implementation, Finance has to be especially attentive to the issue of sunflower management, which can be most damaging in Finance. This calls for a careful formulation of personal measures of success that derive from a desire to be a leader rather than merely a manager.

Finally, speed is especially important in Finance. By taking an option approach to investment decisions, Finance can help speed up an organization without committing excessive resources.

Reflections and Discussion

Organizational Steps for Improving Value Creation in Finance
1. Conduct a survey of those in your Finance group to construct the analog of Table 7.1 for your company. Summarize the lessons that you learn about how those in the group view value creation and the effectiveness of the performance metrics being used for Finance. Develop an action plan to deal with these lessons.
2. Write down your Finance strategy in three bullet points or less. Write a brief paragraph describing how this strategy is consistent with your overall corporate strategy. Be sure to (a) identify the key value drivers to which the strategy is linked and (b) specify the manner in which the strategy takes a multiple-value-creation-perspectives approach that will position Finance more in the Collaborate and Create quadrants.
3. What distinguishes your Finance strategy from those of your competitors? How does your strategy create a sustainable competitive advantage for your organization?
4. List what your Finance organization has done in the last five years to accomplish the following: (a) help the company focus singularly on shareholder value; (b) adopt a single clear definition of value and an associated measure of this value; (c) redesign your company's management information systems to improve the speed of decision making; (d) redesign your company's organization to improve value creation and its visibility to shareholders; and (e) help your company grow. Assess your performance in each dimension and develop a plan to increase your contribution wherever possible.

Personal Steps for Improving Value Creation in Finance
1. Write the ten most important activities you engage in and identify which quadrant each activity predominantly belongs to. Draw a Wholonics profile based on your list. Then draw a *desired* Wholonics profile that makes you an effective strategic partner, business integrator,

and leader. Identify at least three *new* activities you will have to engage in to help move you to the desired profile. Since the total amount of time available is the same as before, you will have to determine which of the ten activities you previously engaged in will be allocated less of your time now. Include in these activities at least one that involves getting to make new friends and the names of those from HR, Marketing, and Sales and New Product Development whom you will get to know better.

2. Write a brief statement of personal strategy that will produce actions on your part to move you to your desired Wholonics profile and that is consistent with the three new activities identified in step 1. Also write a brief paragraph describing how your strategy will distinguish you from others in your organization.

3. Write down your personal measures of success, at least one of which differs from what your organization defines as performance assessment metrics for you. Ask yourself how your personal measures of success help you to overcome sunflower management and be passionately committed to the truth and to a focus on shareholder value.

4. What is your personal vision of value creation and self-fulfillment? List the risky things you have done in the last two years—things that had the potential to cost you your job—to ensure the realization of your vision. How many can you identify? How would you rate yourself on a continuum of 1 (transactional manager) to 5 (leader)? What will you do to improve your score?

5. Do you get tasks accomplished at a rate that surpasses others in your organization? Is your ability to do this improving through time? Develop an action plan to improve your speed, including parallel processing of multiple tasks.

Afterword

ow do you know if you are on your way to being a great value creator? If you've read this far, you'll probably have no trouble answering this question. But underneath all the specifics presented in this book are three simple questions to keep in mind.

- *Are you really having fun in your job?*
  Value creators derive enormous satisfaction from their jobs. They love their work so much that others tend to view them as workaholics. But work is not particularly stressful for them. Is this true for you?

- *Are you making visibly higher value-creation contributions to the organization than your colleagues and being recognized and rewarded for them?*
  If you are a value creator, your output will speak for itself. Don't expect others to always notice the value of your contribution in the short run—but in the long run, your contribution will become visible and be rewarded.

□

- *Are you consistently producing high-quality output at a speed that far exceeds that of others?*
  Value creators are consistently fast *without* compromising the quality of their output. Do you fall in this category?

■

If you are an effective value creator, you know instinctively that you can always get better. Value creation is a journey, not a destination. The many strategies described in this book are essentially variations on a few basic themes. Here they are, in summary form:

- *Continually develop a sharper and more focused definition of value.*
  No matter how advanced you are in your value-creation skills, you can always benefit by introspection about what value means to you and how well your definition fits your current circumstances. By reflecting frequently on what value means to you, you can also improve your focus on maximizing it.

- *Continually refine your personal strategy.*
  There is a lot to be gained by periodically revisiting your three-bullet-point personal strategy statement. Is it focusing your attention on the things you are unique and excellent at? Can it be improved in terms of the guidance it gives you for cutting out those activities that you are merely good (or perhaps incompetent) at? Should it be recalibrated in light of the new opportunities that have come your way recently or the new skills you have developed? These questions are particularly important for value creators, whose ability to handle a multitude of tasks sometimes gives them a "Superman complex." They feel they can do anything! As a result they may take on too many things and lose focus.

- *Continually improve your motivation to derive internal satisfaction.*
  All of us crave external validation of our efforts. The danger, of course, is that this natural human need can cause you to

become too concerned about what others think, often at the expense of your own internal satisfaction. This can have damaging consequences for your development as a leader whose focus is on vision realization rather than successfully completing transactions.

To avoid this effect, periodically examine your own behavior. Reflect on what has been driving you recently to see whether your internal moral compass needs adjustment, whether you need to recommit to the truth and to value creation with even greater passion and conviction.

- *Be a sponge—absorb knowledge from others.*
No matter how well you are creating value, there is always somebody out there doing *something* better than you are. Find out what that something is. Learn what makes those people better at it than you. Discover their "rules" and adapt them to your setting to improve your effectiveness.

Value creation is one of the most satisfying of all human pursuits. Do it well, and you will be in control of your own professional life. You will bring new meaning to your work and to your organization.

■

Based on research that has been done on the rates of return earned on their acquisition investments by successful acquirers as well as the average premium paid in leveraged buyouts, I have estimated that the average publicly traded company can increase its market value by about 30 percent simply by making better value creators out of all its employees. The tools with which to do this have been developed in this book. May you derive true joy and unmatched satisfaction as you begin to use them.

Notes

Chapter 1

1. I would like to thank my colleague E. Han Kim for suggesting the term *sunflower management* for this phenomenon.
2. See J. Edward Russo and Paul J. H. Schoemaker, *Decision Traps: The Ten Barriers to Brilliant Decision-Making and How to Overcome Them* (New York: Simon & Schuster, 1990).
3. For more on this accomplishment, see *Four Hour House* (videotape), available from Building Industry Association, 6336 Greenwich, Suite A, San Diego CA 92122 (619-450-1221).
4. *Wall Street Journal,* October 8, 1999.

Chapter 2

1. See also the article by Shawn Tully, "The Real Key to Creating Shareholder Wealth," *Fortune* (September 20, 1993): 38–50.
2. For a discussion of the model, see Jeff DeGraff, Anjan Thakor, and Robert Quinn, "Eliminating Strategic Blindspots: A Wholonics Approach to Value Creation," University of Michigan Business School working paper, April 2000.

Chapter 3

1. See Andy Reinhardt, "Who Says Intel's Chips Are Down?" *Business Week* (December 7, 1998): 103–104.
2. See Robert D. Hof, "The Education of Andrew Grove," *Business Week* (January 16, 1995): 60–62.
3. See Phillip L. Zweig, Kelley Holland, and Keith Alexander, "Tense Scenes from a Marriage," *Business Week* (January 16, 1995): 66–67. This article describes the Mellon culture as "bean counting and technocratic."
4. See Joseph M. Williams, *Style: Ten Lessons in Clarity and Grace,* 6th ed. (White Plains, N.Y.: Longman, 2000), p. 219.
5. See John Boquist, Todd Milbourn, and Anjan Thakor, *The Value Sphere: Secrets of Creating and Retaining Shareholder Wealth* (Bloomington, Ind.: VIA Press, 1999).

Chapter 4

1. See David P. Hamilton and Steve Glain, "Koreans Move to Grab Memory Chip Market from the Japanese," *Wall Street Journal* (March 14, 1995): A-1, A-8.
2. Hamilton and Glain, "Koreans Move to Grab Memory Chip Market from the Japanese."
3. Hamilton and Glain, "Koreans Move to Grab Memory Chip Market from the Japanese."
4. For a discussion of the pros and cons of organizing product innovation within the firm as opposed to outsourcing it, see Henry W. Chesbrough and David J. Teece, "When Is Virtual Virtuous? Organizing for Innovation," *Harvard Business Review* (January-February 1996): 65–74.
5. See Donald J. Wheeler, *Understanding Variation: The Key to Managing Chaos* (Knoxville, Tenn.: SPC Press, 1993).

Chapter 5

1. See Larry Light, "Now That's a Pepsi Challenge," *Business Week* (May 3, 1999): 151.

2. See Debra Sparks, "Who's Getting More Bang for the Marketing Buck," *Business Week* (May 31, 1999): 148–150.

3. See John Boquist, Todd Milbourn, and Anjan V. Thakor, *The Value Sphere: Secrets of Creating and Retaining Shareholder Wealth* (Bloomington, Ind.: VIA Press, 1999).

4. The problems associated with making inferences based on Table 5.2 are quite clear. First, the table does not tell us anything about the incremental revenues attributable to these companies' marketing expenditures, which is what we need to judge the effectiveness of their marketing outlays. Second, we don't know the lagged relationship between marketing outlays and their effect on revenues—that is, if I spend on marketing today, when will I see its impact on revenue?

5. See Peter Galuszka, Ellen Newborne, and Wendy Zellner, "P&G's Hottest New Product: P&G," *Business Week* (October 5, 1998): 92–96.

6. See J. Edward Russo and Paul H. Schoemaker, *Decision Traps: The Ten Barriers to Brilliant Decision-Making and How to Overcome Them* (New York: Simon & Schuster, 1990).

7. See Peter Burrows, Ira Sager, and Michael Moeller, "Can Compaq Catch Up?" *Business Week* (May 3, 1999): 162–165.

8. This case study is based on David Baron and David Besanko, "Strategy, Organization, and Incentives: Global Corporate Banking at Citibank," working paper, Stanford University and Northwestern University, March 1999.

9. *CCInvestor,* June 1996.

10. See Paul C. Judge, "High Techstar," *Cover Story* no. 3620 (March 15, 1999): 72.

11. See Nanette Byrnes, "How Schwab Grabbed the Lion's Share," *Business Week* (June 28, 1999): 88.

Chapter 6

1. See Larry Light, "Man on the Spot," *Business Week* (May 3, 1999): 142–151.

2. See Michael Moeller, Steven Hamm, and Timothy J. Mullaney, "Remaking Microsoft," *Business Week* (May 17, 1999): 108–114.

3. Moeller, Hamm, and Mullaney, "Remaking Microsoft."
4. See John Byrne, "The Corporation of the Future," *Business Week* (August 31, 1998): 102–106.
5. Tricon Annual Report, 1998.
6. This case is based on the discussion in Al Ehrbar, *EVA: The Real Key to Creating Wealth* (New York: Wiley, 1998).

Chapter 7

1. See Barbara Minto, *The Minto Pyramid Principle* (London: Minto International, 1996).
2. See Richard Farson, *Management of the Absurd: Paradoxes in Leadership* (New York: Simon & Schuster, 1996).
3. See Frances X. Frie, Patrick T. Harker, and Larry W. Hunter, "Inside the Black Box: What Makes a Bank Efficient?" Financial Institution Center WP 97–20, The Wharton School, April 1997.
4. This case is based on J. Dial and Kevin J. Murphy, "Incentives, Downsizing, and Value Creation at General Dynamics," *Journal of Financial Economics* 37, no. 3 (1995): 261–314.
5. Peter Carlson, "Chairman of the Bucks," *Washington Post Magazine* (April 5, 1992): 15.
6. Alison Leigh Cowan, "The Gadfly CEOs Want to Swat," *New York Times* (February 2, 1992).
7. See Ian Springsteel and Roy Harris, "Birth of a Salesman," *CFO Magazine* (June 1997).
8. See *CFO Magazine* (October 1999): 44.
9. See Linda Grant, "GE's `Smart Bomb' Strategy", *Fortune* (July 21, 1997): 109–110.
10. The theory behind strategic market entry decisions with real options is developed in Arnoud Boot, Todd Milbourn, and Anjan Thakor, "Evolution of Organizational Scale and Scope: Does It Ever Pay to Get Bigger and Become Less Focused?" working paper, University of Michigan, 1999.

The Author

Anjan V. Thakor holds the Edward J. Frey Professorship of Banking and Finance at the University of Michigan Business School. Prior to joining the faculty there, he served as the NBD Professor of Finance and chairman of the Finance Department at the School of Business at Indiana University. Anjan has also served on the faculties of Northwestern University and UCLA as a visiting professor.

Anjan designs and teaches courses in the Ph.D. and MBA programs and at the Business School's Executive Education Center. His executive education courses include "Growth Strategies," "Corporate Financial Management," and "Mergers, Acquisitions, and Divestitures." His research and teaching interests focus on corporate finance and banking. In addition to his many published articles, monographs, and book chapters, he has written two books besides the present volume: *The Value Sphere: Secrets of Creating and Retaining Shareholder Wealth* (VIA Press, 1999) and *Contemporary Financial Intermediation* (Dryden Press, 1994). He currently serves as managing editor of *Journal of Financial Intermediation* and associate editor of *Journal of Banking and Finance, Financial Management,* and *Journal of Small Business Finance.* He

247

has served on the Nominating Committee for the Nobel Prize in Economics since 1993.

Anjan is actively involved in corporate consultancy, an executive education, including extensive work in corporate finance and banking. He has helped various types of organizations, including numerous Fortune 500 firms, navigate the complexities of financing, capital investment, and performance evaluation for strategic decision making. Clients include Citigroup, Reuters, CIGNA, Whirlpool, Dana, RR Donnelley, Anheuser-Busch, The Limited, Ryder Integrated Logistics, Zenith Industrial, Lincoln National, Waxman Industries, Landscape Structures, Allison Engine, Borg-Warner Automotive, and AT&T.

Index

Net present value (NPV), 132, 133, 138–139
Networks, electronic, 189–188
New product development: business strategy for, 149–154; desired evolution in Wholonics perspective, 148; developing speed in, 157–158; and explosion of spending by e-commerce companies, 137–141; geographic focus in, *versus* brand or product focus, 141–142; ignoring breakthroughs in sales and distribution in, 146–148; improving value creation in, 131–162; meaning of value in, 132–137, 160; organizational steps for improving value creation in, 163–164; organizational success strategies for, 158–159; personal measure of success in, 155–157; personal steps for improving value creation in, 164; personal success strategies for, 159–162; and reluctance to cannibalize, 142–146; role of, in creation of value, 135; traditional positioning of in create quadrant of Wholonics model, 137–148
Nike, 201
Nonprofit community service organizations, 3–4, 8–9
Not-invented-here syndrome, 115, 123

O
Opportunity cost, 9
Organizational culture, 99–100
Organizational expectations, 96–97
Outcomes: from desired, to resource allocation, 72; value drivers *versus*, 10–11; visible, produced by value creators, 5–6
Outsourcing, 14, 16
Overconfidence bias, 145
Overengineering, 115. *See also* Engineering mentality
Overoptimism bias, 145

P
Parallel processing, 99–100, 100–102; sequential processing *versus*, 101
PepsiCo, 131, 166, 170, 202
Percival, J., 222

Personal success, 21–22
Personal value added (PVA), 43
Peters, T., 24, 80
P&G. *See* Procter & Gamble
Philips, 141
Pillsbury, 232
Pizza Hut, 189–191
P&L. *See* Profit and loss responsibility
Pottruck, D., 158
Prentice, G. D., 79
Process improvement, *versus* product innovations, 115
Process redesign, 97–99
Procter & Gamble (P&G), 18, 141, 142
Procurement: and overview of procurement function, 107–109; personal success strategies for, 126–127; research findings for, 108–109; role of, in value creation, 110; self-interest in, 108; strategy disconnects in, 118–120; traditional positioning of, in control quadrant of Wholonics model, 112–118
Product decisions, poor, 115–116, 144
Product focus: *versus* geographic focus, 141–142; in marketing, 146–148
Profit and loss (P&L) responsibility, 170–171
PVA. *See* Personal value added
Pyramid Principle, 208, 209

Q
Quaker Oats, 49–51
Quality, and speed, 25

R
Randazzo, R., 195
Reorganization, finance driven, 215–216
Resource allocation, from desired outcomes to, 72
Reuters, 215–216
Revenue, 9
Revlon, 146
Rewards, 87–88, 98. *See also* Sunflower management
Rice-A-Roni, 49
RoadRailer (Wabash National), 122–123
Ruettgers, M. C., 152–155
Ryan, T., 195

for, 105; power of, 17; situational,
76
Strategy disconnects: from decision
making, 77–80; in manufacturing,
118–119; in procurement, 118–120
Suboptimization, 50
Success: defining and measuring,
86–97; measurement of, 19–24; sunflower management and, 21–22
Success, personal measure of: in finance, 225–228; in human resources,
181–186; in marketing, 155–157; in
new product development, 155–157;
in sales and distribution, 155–157
Success strategies, organizational: for
finance, 232–233; for marketing,
158–159; for new product development, 158–159; for sales and distribution, 158–159
Success strategies, personal: for finance, 233–235; for human resources,
194–196; for manufacturing, 126–
127; for marketing, 159–162; for
new product development, 159–
162; for procurement, 126–127; for
sales and distribution, 159–162
Sunbeam Corporation, 32
Sunflower management, 21–22; organizational and personal understanding of, 23–24; organizational
tools for minimizing, 87–93; personal tools for minimizing, 93–97
Superman complex, 240

T
Taco Bell, 189–191
Team players, 21
Tech Data, 146
Tenneco Automotive, 195
Thailand, 118
Thakor, A., 82
The Limited, 208
Toshiba, 113
Total Quality Management (TQM), 57,
127
TQM. *See* Total Quality Management
Travelers, 174
Tricon, 188–191
Trust, development of, 90–91, 94. *See
also* Sunflower management

U
Unilever, 141
United Kingdom, 232
United States automobile industry,
143
United States Navy, 217
University of Michigan, 174
UPS, 72, 73

V
Value: destruction of, by mutual
agreement, 49–50; organizational
steps for achieving shared understanding of, 65–66; personal steps
for improving understanding of,
66–67
Value, definition of: and focus on
value creation, 32–52; lack of, and
understanding of value drivers,
32–43; main impediments to, 33; organizational strategy for, 38; personal strategy for, 38–39
Value, Economic (performance metric), 3, 6, 9, 33, 53, 72, 74, 165,
207–208, 232
Value, meaning of: in finance, 202–
206; in human resources, 167–172;
importance of understanding, 6–9;
in marketing, 132–137; in new
product development, 132–137; to
organization, 6–13; in sales and distribution, 132–137; two levels of
understanding, 9–13
Value creation: activities for, 13–17;
definition of, 2–4; improving, in finance, 233–234; improving, in
human resources, 192–193; improving, in marketing, 131–162; improving, in new product development,
131–162; improving, in sales and
distribution, 131–162; as journey
versus destination, 26–27; mastery
of speed in, 24–26; and meaning of
value, 6–13; multiple perspectives
on, 13–17; organizational steps for,
28–29; personal measure of success
in, 19–24; personal steps for, 29–30;
personal strategy for linking decision making to, 84–86; role of
human resources in, 169; role of